Running IT like a Business

A Step-by-Step Guide
to Accenture's Internal IT

Running IT like a Business

A Step-by-Step Guide
to Accenture's Internal IT

Second edition

ROBERT E. KRESS

IT Governance Publishing

IT Governance Publishing
IT Governance Limited
Unit 3, Clive Court
Bartholomew's Walk
Cambridgeshire Business Park
Ely
Cambridgeshire
CB7 4EH
United Kingdom

www.itgovernance.co.uk

First published in the United Kingdom in 2011
by IT Governance Publishing.

ISBN 978-1-84928-356-4 second edition 2012
(ISBN 978-1-84928-308-3 first edition)

PREFACE

Information technology (IT) has, over the past half-century, migrated from being a specialized technical discipline staffed by computer scientists, to the position it occupies today at the very center of enterprise capabilities and assets. Regardless of industry sector or geographic location, running a company, a governmental agency, or an enterprise of any other kind has, quite simply, become inconceivable without the technologies, skills and resources found in the typical IT function. In many instances, IT is not only an enabler of productive activity on a vast scale, but a source of differentiation and competitive advantage.

The IT function in a typical corporation can employ hundreds or even thousands of professionals, and account for up to 10% or more of net revenue in annual spending. No major initiative of any kind can be effectively implemented without detailed preparation of the IT infrastructure and the applications required to support the program. Given the immense importance that IT has assumed in the life of an enterprise, it is unsurprising that mastering the management of an IT organization has become as important as mastering the technology itself.

The centrality of IT as a tool for every organization provides the rationale for this book. If a professionally run IT function is essential to every business, government or non-profit enterprise, then running IT like a business is the only logical way to run IT. This has been our approach at Accenture since our company was established. Rather than treating IT strictly as a service function or cost center, we have chosen to apply the same rigorous management disciplines to our internal IT capability as we do to managing the rest of our business. In so doing, we have accumulated a body of policies and practices that have been tested over time and have proved their worth. We are pleased to share these insights with our colleagues throughout the IT community in the interest of advancing the professionalism of IT as a discipline, and to highlight the indispensable value of IT as a contributor to high performance in an enterprise.

This book presents not my IT story, but Accenture's story, and I am privileged to share it. I have had the honor of working with an absolutely superb team of IT professionals at Accenture throughout my career, and I am grateful to them all for the many things they have taught me along the way. So I extend a special thanks to my colleagues around the world who work inside Accenture's internal IT function – which we refer to as the Accenture CIO Organization.

At Accenture, we believe that we have one of the best IT organizations in the world. Who knows if this is true? There are talented IT professionals working day after day in enterprises large and small. I have had opportunities to meet many IT colleagues at other companies and enterprises, and I am always impressed by their commitment to their profession, by the energy they devote to their work, and by their willingness to make sacrifices for the people they serve. There is, of course, no way of definitively saying who is best. So let it suffice to say that we aspire to be the best. There can be nothing wrong with such an aspiration, and it is one that I am sure we share with all our colleagues across the IT industry.

ABOUT THE AUTHOR

Robert E. Kress is the chief operating officer (COO) of Accenture's high-performance IT organization, which supports and advances the business goals of a $22 billion company with more than 215,000 employees in 52 different countries. Reporting directly to Accenture's chief information officer, Bob has overall responsibility for running IT like a business. He manages the organization's global IT operation with its $700 million annual budget – his roles including the direct management of IT governance, strategy, planning, risk management, supplier and contract management, audits and IT policy, as well as communications, business performance, finance, human resources (HR), deployable resources and organizational development.

Bob has extensive experience in IT planning, governance, technology operations, application development, product management, service planning and program management. Before joining the IT operation, Bob was an Accenture consultant. In that role, he developed and delivered large and complex IT transformation projects and business solutions that maximized return on investment for clients in the healthcare, government and consumer products sectors.

Bob's first book, *IT Governance to Drive High Performance: Lessons from Accenture,* was published in 2010.

Bob holds a Bachelor of Science degree in physics from Loras College in Dubuque, Iowa, and a Master of Business Administration degree from the University of Iowa. He resides in the Chicago area with his wife and children. He enjoys gardening and attending sporting events with his family.

ACKNOWLEDGEMENTS

We would like to acknowledge the following reviewers of this book for their useful contributions: Chris Evans, ICT Compliance Manager, London Fire Brigade; ir H.L. (Maarten) Souw RE, IT Auditor, UWV; and Antonio Velasco, CEO, Sinersys Technologies.

CONTENTS

Contents

INTRODUCTION

Over the course of my career (and perhaps yours as well), IT has undergone successive waves of disruptive, even radical, transformation.

If you started working in IT in the 1980s, you would have seen the earliest minicomputers beginning to appear alongside mainframes. Hard-wired enterprise IT networks were beginning to make tapes, disks and other physical media obsolete. Assembler and COBOL[1] were still around, but more and more code was being written in Fortran, PL/1[2] and Pascal.

By the 1990s, IT working environments were upended by AS/400 units and the first PCs. Computer platforms were evolving from being one-per-company to one-per-location, and eventually to one-per-person. We started using relational databases, and the first mobile telephones appeared. Remember how cool everyone thought those brick-like satellite cell phones were, despite their weight and bulk?

At the turn of the century, PCs and laptops had taken over, the Internet was spreading faster than you could say, "dot com," the computer languages of choice were Visual Basic, JavaScript, and the C/C+/C++ triumvirate, and cell phones were shrinking as fast as they were spreading.

As each of these waves of technical innovation roiled the IT industry, a potentially even more profound organizational

---

[1] Common Business-Oriented Language
[2] Programming Language One

transformation was slowly but surely taking place behind the technology headlines.

In the early days of IT, the corporate world was divided into two parts: "line" and "staff". Everyone who worked in IT was thought of as being on the "staff" side of the business: part of a support function – not unlike "facilities," in that we were part of the working infrastructure required to support the enterprise we served. And "serve" *was* the operative word. Line executives told us what they needed, and our job was to go out and make it happen.

As IT became more important to the fortunes and the future of organizations, things began to change. In at least some enterprises, IT professionals came to be recognized as making strategic contributions to the enterprises they served, whether these were corporations, government bodies, non-profit organizations, or other enterprises.

This improvement in the standing of IT has been real and meaningful, but uneven. In some enterprises, IT today is regarded as a full strategic partner and player. In just as many others, the IT team retains an unfortunate and undeserved second-class status.

What can IT professionals do to help ensure that every IT function and IT professional receives the respect and support they deserve? Clearly, we must always strive to be as technically proficient as possible – capable of leveraging the enormous power of technology for the benefit of the organizations we serve. We must be knowledgeable about the latest technological innovations, and responsive to the changing challenges in our enterprises. But technical proficiency, in itself, is insufficient to win IT a place at the decision-making table – which is the position we need to hold in order to maximize IT's contribution to our organizations.

If IT is going to be recognized as a fully capable business partner by the businesses and organizations we serve, we need to think like business people, we need to act as our counterparts in "line" businesses act, and we need to understand and speak the language of business, not just the language of technology.

In short, if IT professionals want to be included in strategic discussions at the highest levels of our businesses and other organizations, we need to run IT like a business. Only in this way will our colleagues in other disciplines understand how IT functions, appreciate the value that IT delivers, and be prepared to support the investments in IT that will be required to allow our companies and enterprises to operate at high levels.

As a member of the IT leadership team at Accenture, I have had the opportunity to study firsthand, over the past 10 years, what it means to run IT like a business. Accenture is a global management consulting, technology services and outsourcing company. Today, we have more than 215,000 people serving clients in more than 120 countries, and we are being supported by an internal IT function that we call the Accenture CIO Organization. When Accenture was established as a new enterprise at the beginning of the last decade, our heritage as both business consultants and technological innovators instinctively compelled us to approach IT operations with a business mindset. Within Accenture's corporate culture, information technology was never an esoteric endeavor that no one else understood; our company was filled with IT experts, and each one of them was quite prepared to tell us how to do our jobs –

technology being one of the major services we provide to a world-class roster of clients. So we fully anticipated that our colleagues in the business would understand everything that we in IT were doing, and would expect to see a strong business rationale for every move we made. We knew, from the beginning, that our colleagues in other parts of the business would expect to see Accenture's return on a major investment in IT, and so, at a very early stage, we began thinking about metrics and measurements. In short, we did not have much choice other than to run IT like a business.

So, turning necessity into a virtue, we began to assemble the necessary principles and policies. In retrospect, the process outlined in the pages of this book may appear predictable, and success even inevitable. In practice, our experience was closer to that of a laboratory experiment, with a considerable amount of trial and error. In successive chapters, I attempt to set forth in logical fashion our most important discoveries. Beginning with IT strategy and governance, we explore the foundations of running IT like a business. We then examine why managed services proved to be so central to an effective approach. After looking, in Chapter 3, at the critical roles played by performance measurements and metrics in tracking and validating IT operations, we explore the many opportunities for value creation that we pursued and that are available to virtually every IT function. We then discuss topics of special relevance to IT operations, and examine how running IT like a business can contribute to high performance across the entire enterprise. In the final chapter, we document the actual long-term results Accenture was able to derive from our decade-long transformational journey.

I close each chapter with what may, at first, strike the reader as a contradictory or counter-intuitive finding. The most valuable lessons in business, as in life, are not always the logical ones. As we made our way down the transformative path of Accenture's IT, we kept coming across unexpected lessons we had learned, and so now we pass these along to others who seek to take a similar path.

Inside Accenture, we always had an intrinsic faith that running IT like a business made good business sense. Only now, after 10 years of difficult but exciting change, do we fully appreciate the transformative power unleashed when you operate your IT function just as you would any business. What we discovered was that it is precisely when you *refuse* to treat IT differently, and apply to IT operations the same disciplines and rigor that successful managers bring to the management of any business, that you unchain IT's ability to change an enterprise powerfully, rapidly and repeatedly.

When we set out on our journey, we expected to change a few things here and there. But when we had reached our destination, and looked back at the territory we had traversed and the path we had followed, we discovered that we had changed absolutely everything.

So the story of running IT like a business at Accenture is really a story about transforming IT from top to bottom. As you map your own IT journey, we trust that the lessons we share here will be of some benefit to you.

CHAPTER 1: IT STRATEGY AND GOVERNANCE

When you want to run IT like a business, where do you start? Is it as simple as charging out the IT staff's time to internal customers? Some IT executives, hoping to demonstrate business value to executive leadership sponsors, do precisely that. But if running IT like a business amounts to nothing more than a chargeback system, you risk missing the quintessential ingredient of any successful business: understanding your customers' needs and meeting those needs better than the available alternatives can.

If an IT function is going to transform its identity from cost center to value center, something more will be required. As I will argue throughout this book, running IT like a business demands a change in mindset as much as a change in specific business processes. This transformation of attitude has many distinct dimensions, which we will examine in subsequent chapters. Developing IT strategy and IT governance are the first and arguably the two most important steps on the journey toward a new way of organizing internal IT.

Start with strategy

IT strategy informs what you are trying to accomplish at a very basic level. Before you can decide what to do with your IT function, you need to understand the business environment in which you are operating. What is the overall strategy of your enterprise, and how is your business or organization trying to achieve it? Is your business strategy to be the low-cost provider of a commodity, the high-value provider of a highly specialized service, or something in between? Is your business strategy predicated on making a large number of acquisitions? In such a case, the rapid and smooth integration of those external acquisitions into your internal operations becomes a critical criterion for success. Suppose your business strategy aims to expand the enterprise beyond a few core markets: this would place a premium on technology platforms that could start small, but scale up easily as you grow.

There are few limits to the variety of business strategies out there in the real world. To know your company's strategy in detail, is to know what underlying business mission your IT strategy must successfully support in order to be effective.

By way of illustration, Accenture's business strategy is to collaborate with our clients to help them become high-performance businesses and governments by leveraging our global management consulting, technology services and outsourcing solutions on their behalf. Since our client base includes many of the world's largest global enterprises, our strategy as a business is to deliver the same consistent high performance to our clients, no matter what part of the world we are in.

This business strategy has exerted a significant influence on our IT strategy over the past decade. Early in our still-young corporate history, we decided that we would need to operate information technology in a highly centralized and globally consistent way, in order to support the larger business strategy of the company. Accenture's three major businesses – management consulting, technology and outsourcing – are different in many respects, but all three rely on shared, global business processes. So it made sense for us to strive for a single global technology footprint, governed by a single overarching and centralized IT governance structure.

We broadly refer to this IT strategy as Accenture's "Theme of One." Wherever feasible, we standardize, consolidate, and strive to come as close as possible to a single instance of every technology tool we use. Admittedly, the Theme of One is only our vision of an ideal technology environment, and the ideal is not always achieved in the real world of practical business. Nevertheless, we aim high and expect to approximate that vision wherever we can.

At the same time, Accenture's business operations span many industries in every geographic market. This diversity dictates that our IT strategy must also have a high degree of built-in flexibility, enabling our IT operating model to align with Accenture's go-to-market strategy, so that we can more effectively support the varying needs of internal customers. To complement the standardization implicit in the Theme of One approach, Accenture's IT strategy has a second and equally strong managed services component, which literally puts the decision-making power about IT services in the hands of our customers. We accomplish this at Accenture through a variety of mechanisms, which will be explored in greater detail in Chapter 2. At this stage, it will be sufficient to note that, in our IT strategy, the global scope of Accenture's Theme of One is counterbalanced by the ability our internal customers possess to select the IT service levels that are appropriate for their business needs.

A third component of Accenture's IT strategy relates to Accenture's global footprint and its ability to tap deep technology resources from a range of low-cost locations around the world. Accenture currently employs more than

50,000 technology professionals in India alone – a number that is growing all the time. We also employ large contingents of technology professionals working in markets from Argentina to the Philippines. Our access to superior technology professionals based in markets with highly cost-effective labor rates gives us an attractive opportunity to leverage lower-cost resources for the benefit of our internal customers. Even more importantly, using variable resources that support multiple clients allows us greater access to people with unique skills necessary to support our IT function. We may not need a full-time worker with specific skills on a permanent basis: "sharing" a variable resource provides an excellent solution.

So our IT strategy includes an explicit goal of centering our workforce on variable resources in low-cost locations. Hardly surprising for a company that ranks among the leading providers of outsourcing services in the world, Accenture itself includes a sizable outsourcing component in its IT strategy. We effectively outsource a significant portion of our own internal IT operations to market-facing Accenture outsourcing specialists around the world, who can provide the same high-quality services as our own IT professionals, but at a more attractive cost.

Accenture's IT operations, at the time of this writing, employ some 4,000 IT professionals. Only about 500 of those individuals – that's one in eight – are full-time employees of our IT function. The remainder of our team consists of Accenture IT professionals who work in Accenture's network of low-cost delivery centers, IT specialists we share with our infrastructure outsourcing business, and Accenture consultants seconded to our function from other parts of the business. The result is that

Accenture's IT function has a much lower percentage of permanent resources than many other companies have.

To round out the key elements of Accenture's IT strategy, we incorporate rigorous performance processes into everything we do. We communicate extensively about major initiatives to internal customers, as well as to client colleagues in IT who wonder, "Well, how does Accenture handle this issue?"

So Accenture's IT strategy includes seven key elements:

- Creating strong, central IT governance
- Aligning the IT operating model with Accenture's go-to-market strategy
- Running IT like a business based on a managed-services approach
- Consolidating, standardizing and centralizing operations
- Focusing the workforce strategy on variable resources and low-cost locations
- Strengthening IT performance measurement processes
- Communicating successes and benefits realization at every opportunity.

Effective strategies are organic and integrated, rather than a series of isolated bullet points, but this list begins to define what we inside Accenture's IT function mean when we discuss IT strategy.

Developing your IT strategy

How do *you* develop an IT strategy if your enterprise does not presently have one? How do you correct or re-launch an IT strategy that may have been detoured by economic conditions or external circumstances? How do you keep your IT strategy aligned with your business, as the business changes and evolves over time?

We have already discussed the critical importance of having a clear understanding of your business strategy. This will serve as a foundation for determining the appropriate IT strategy. IT does not function in a vacuum, but exists to serve the needs of the business. What are the priorities and goals being pursued by your business enterprise? Are these priorities changing in response to market opportunities or pressures? What objectives is the business pursuing that IT is uniquely qualified to help it achieve?

If these are some of the questions you might ask as you begin to think seriously about IT strategy, where do you find the answers? When the topic is strategy of any kind, some people instinctively reach for some blank sheets of paper, lock themselves in a room for a few days, and hope that – through a process of arduous soul-searching – they will emerge with a strategy.

Our experience at Accenture is precisely the opposite: effective strategy emerges from a dynamic dialogue and interaction with your business at many levels. Only by talking in depth to leaders and internal customers throughout your business is it possible to develop a clear sense of where your business is heading and how the IT function may be able to help it get there better, faster and cheaper.

So if IT strategy is new to you, start with wide-ranging discussions and data gathering, so you can inform yourself about the essential issues: What is the current business strategy? From where do we expect growth to come, what are the opportunities for expansion, and where are the challenges and threats to our revenues or profits?

At Accenture, we begin these discussions within the IT function, and then we expand the discussions to involve our senior leaders – including the chief operating officers of our major business units and the account leads on our largest accounts. We seek to hear from them firsthand about their most pressing priorities, and value their perspective on how they think technology may be able to help. Cross-disciplinary discussions with colleagues outside the IT function are indispensable for the development of mature, sophisticated IT strategy. Seek out the business leaders in your enterprise who have direct contact with clients and customers, who confront competitors every business day, and who have an intuitive feel for the way your company's industry is evolving. Interrogate them about their specific strategy for their part of the business, and don't be afraid to ask them what the key "pain points" are that they are living with today, and what technologies you can provide that will make their lives easier. When you engage these executives in the strategic planning process, you will begin to acquire a set of pragmatic business insights that you will need as inputs for your IT strategy. Coincidentally, these same discussions will send a powerful message to business colleagues: that your IT function is there to serve *them*. Your commitment to meeting their needs will pay dividends when you need their support for your IT initiatives.

Alongside the business issues, strategy development also needs to involve an examination of the technological opportunities. Strategic insights can come by taking your research beyond the borders of the enterprise and into the wider technology community. What are the prevailing trends in information technology? What exists today, what is on the near or far horizon, and can we take advantage of those innovations by matching them against business objectives?

At Accenture, we take a hard look at what is happening in the marketplace by making inquiries through as many channels as we can possibly find. Discussions with Accenture's go-to-market technology experts and with professionals at our innovation centers are a valuable source of information. We also track important technology breakthroughs and assess the competitive landscape, paying particular attention to the innovations coming out of Cisco, Hewlett-Packard, Microsoft and other technology giants working alongside us.

Lastly, we have direct access to the Accenture Technology Labs. Their brief is to work on the leading edge of technological change, wherever it may take them – which keeps them especially well-informed about the "next new thing" across an extraordinarily wide spectrum of industries and disciplines. In addition to the preparation of an annual technology forecast, Accenture Technology Labs support teams of scientists and technologists who are dedicated to exploring and exploiting technology for practical applications. In the process of doing so, they leverage IT in imaginative new ways, all of which inform and enrich our understanding of the possibilities that lie ahead.

On both the business side and the technology side, we take the strategic investigation inside Accenture one step further, engaging our 215,000-strong workforce in the discussions on innovative collaboration technologies. In this way, we aim to tap the wisdom of crowds – in this case the crowds of technologically savvy Accenture professionals working in industries and markets around the world. Since our global enterprise seeks to hire the most proficient consultants and technologists it can find, it only makes sense to take advantage of the vast information-gathering power of this global team. Using collaborative tools, such as Accenture's Innovation Grapevine, we seed ideas about emerging trends and technologies in shared electronic workspaces. We then invite everyone to comment on the merits of existing ideas, or to put forward new ideas, with the expectation that the brightest insights will invariably rise to the surface.

A smart IT strategy blends the best insights from these two independent and mutually supportive investigations, marrying insights into where the business is heading with a keen understanding of where technology could take us. The result is an IT strategy with two distinct components: IT business strategy and IT technology strategy. At Accenture, we visualize our IT strategy in the following way:

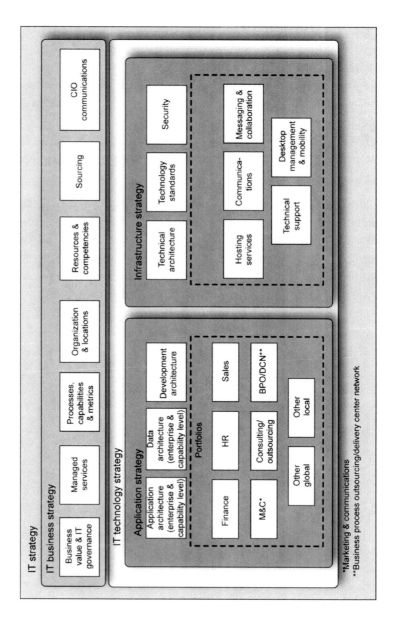

Figure 1: Accenture's IT strategy

Although somewhat unusual, thinking about IT strategy in terms of these two broad clusters of platforms, solutions, capabilities and services can be productive. In too many enterprises, IT is viewed simplistically as the necessary evil: an expensive cost center instead of a lucrative value center, and a big headache rather than a big opportunity. The price for such a distorted view of IT comes in the opportunities that are missed: when you are not looking at the power technology can bring to bear, you are never going to see the full value of your IT investment. Of course, IT functions in certain industries have shed these mischaracterizations; banks and financial service firms simply would not be able to function today without IT. The same must be said for most major manufacturing enterprises.

Grounding your IT function in a firm foundation of IT strategy is a vital first step toward securing the full recognition of IT's worth across the enterprise. It is important to have your strategy well-documented, and to make certain that people at all levels of your IT function understand its implications. The strategy can only be as good as the people who implement it. In complex IT functions, people at several levels are making daily business decisions that have a direct bearing on IT strategy. For this reason, it is essential to communicate the strategy and to ensure that it is understood at the leadership level as well as all other major levels, because you want daily decisions to be made in the context of the broader IT strategy.

Putting together a coherent and comprehensive IT strategy for the first time is no small endeavor. The good news is that, in most enterprises, it is not an annual exercise. At Accenture, we review and update our IT strategy every 18 to 24 months. At the beginning of each review, we do not throw the entire IT strategy out and start over, but rather focus on particular areas that need to be refreshed. Strategic continuity is important, particularly because most large IT initiatives can extend over multiple fiscal years (FY). For this reason, it is important to strike an appropriate balance between stability and change.

IT governance

If IT strategy provides the "what," IT governance provides the "how." IT governance sets out who the players are, who is going to make the decisions, and who is going to be held accountable for results.

IT governance creates the institutional structures required for making central investment recommendations to the company or enterprise. At the center is the IT steering committee, where decision makers determine what technology is going to be provided to support the business. Investment decisions, however, are only one aspect of the steering committee's contribution. After the decision to invest in a particular technology is made, the IT steering committee plays a critical role in promoting the necessary buy-in required for programs that entail changes to the organization.

IT governance answers the question: how are we going to manage our IT operation? Effective IT governance is principally an issue of alignment – getting the IT strategy aligned with the business strategy, having the right people lined up to make the necessary decisions, and aligning IT spending with critical business priorities.

Mirroring your corporate structure

Your IT governance structure should mirror the way your enterprise works and align with how overall governance functions in your company.

It is unlikely, for example, that a highly centralized IT governance structure will work in a highly decentralized enterprise; in such a situation, you are more likely to find advantages in a federated model of management than in a single decision-making mechanism. On the other hand, totally centralized IT governance is no panacea. Even a powerful central CIO function needs a governing body with representatives from different parts of the business. This way, deliberation can result in nuanced decision-making, which can, in turn, drive common processes and improve cost-efficiencies at scale across the entire enterprise. Effective governance, in this setting, may enable the enterprise to take advantage of common infrastructure on the lower levels of the technology stack – where commoditization prevails. It may also support different applications at higher levels of the stack – where business divisions or subsidiaries require them.

One enterprise I had the opportunity to study operated 17 distinct data centers in one geographical region. This was because each department within the overall organization ran as a standalone function, and so each function required its own individual data center. Such a situation might call for a decentralized IT governance structure, but certainly presents opportunities for cost reduction through centralization. Devising the right IT governance structure for your enterprise will require trial-and-error experimentation, and the following key roles should be included:

- The IT steering committee, which has the authority to review, endorse and commit funds for IT investment
- Stakeholders, who own opportunities representing changes in business capabilities.
- Sponsors, who are stewards of business capabilities and applications, whether global, regional or local
- The CIO and his or her organization, which includes all the executives who will be held accountable for IT capabilities.

Figure 2: Key roles in IT governance

The IT governance structure at Accenture includes all of these positions, as well as a fifth group – the Accenture Global Management Committee – which includes senior corporate executives who can provide IT investment funding guidance. Our IT steering committee includes the chief operating officers of all our business units *(see Figure 3).*

Operating groups	Growth platforms	Corporate functions and geographic services
• Products COO • Health & Public Service COO • Resources COO • Financial Services COO • Communications, Media & Technology COO.	• Management Consulting COO • Business Process Outsourcing COO • Technology COO • Technology CTO.	• Finance COO • Human Resources COO • Geographic Services COO.

Figure 3: Accenture IT Steering Committee representatives

Responsibilities for IT governance are distributed across these various roles, with specific parties being either directly responsible, participatory, consulted, informed, or accountable for results. These responsibilities include:

- Strategy and structure – including the formulation of IT strategy, enterprise architecture and IT standards
- Multi-year planning of initiatives, product and service plans, and the IT sourcing plan for the enterprise
- Annual planning of priorities, initiatives, the operating plan/budget and capital plan/budget
- Execution – which includes implementation, variations to the plan, performance targets and plans, and benefits realization.

Prioritizing IT investments

As the list suggests, the process of making decisions about IT investments is central to the IT governance process. In any given year, Accenture generates nearly 200 requests for IT investment. The process by which the CIO and the IT steering committee winnow down these requests to identify fundable initiatives illustrates IT governance in action.

Our process gets underway seven to eight months in advance of our fiscal year, when IT executives sit down with business sponsors and begin to identify potential investment areas. In this early stage of the process, the emphasis is on idea generation. Costs and benefits are roughly estimated, rather than precisely calculated.

The IT leadership team then goes through the outputs from these early thoughts to identify duplicative projects, common opportunities and major trends and themes, which are then presented in summary form to the IT steering committee. Before detailed planning begins, there needs to be a general consensus and level of support for the major initiatives.

Typically 180 to 220 proposed programs enter this process of consideration, but only half to two thirds will emerge from it. Once the short list of initiatives has been determined, detailed planning begins to estimate one-time costs, ongoing costs, hard and/or soft benefits, and timelines for development and implementation. Business cases are assembled for each initiative.

After the detailed planning is complete, the IT steering committee divides into sub-committees, one for each of five portfolio areas. Each sub-committee reviews requests in its respective portfolio, preparing laddered lists of investment requests with scores. The laddered rankings from the five areas are then merged into a consolidated ranking for review with the full IT steering committee – the chief operating officers of each of our business units. IT investment funding establishes a value line on the ranking of proposed programs; initiatives above the line are approved, and those below are deferred.

The beauty of the IT steering committee structure lies in its ability to get senior people involved. At Accenture, we hold the sponsor of an initiative responsible for the entire business case, all the way to the realization of the benefits promised. Since IT change usually involves process redesign and organizational changes as well as changes to the underlying technology, you must have a business sponsor responsible for the entire change process. This accountability even extends to outsourcing arrangements, in which the sponsor of the initiative still must be responsible and accountable for the technology.

Once investment allocations for the year have been made, some flexibility should be reserved for opportunities and for changes during the fiscal period covered by your budget. At Accenture, we set aside a hold-back amount precisely for things that might come up during the year. If something important arises, we can also go back to the IT steering committee to request that some project of lesser priority be halted in order to free up funds for the new project.

Investment portfolios

What are "investment portfolios" in the context of an IT operation, and why do we use them? When Accenture's IT function first created the IT governance structure described above, we found that our IT investment decisions tended to become concentrated, year after year, in internal operations. For example, more than 75% of our investments in new IT programs in fiscal year 2005 were for the support of internal corporate function operations. However, the participation of chief operating officers at business units in our IT governance process brought to the fore the IT needs of client-facing sales and delivery teams. To ameliorate a natural bias toward funding internal operations, we developed the concept of investment portfolios, and defined five broad areas:

- Investments designed to support individual business units
- Company-wide investments affecting everyone and everything in Accenture
- Corporate functions – such as human resources or finance
- Investments in pure IT functions
- Investments directly dictated by legal and regulatory requirements.

The effect of this modification in our governance model was striking: by fiscal year 2008 – only three years later – investments in internal operations had shrunk to 34%, while investments in client-facing sales and delivery initiatives had soared to over 40% of total annual investments *(see Figure 4)*. Since then, the share of annual IT investments going to client-facing parts of Accenture's business has continued to climb. The conclusions are obvious. When forced by defined structures of IT governance to consider the broader needs of the business, we suddenly discovered much better ways to invest the company's funds and to improve IT operations simultaneously.

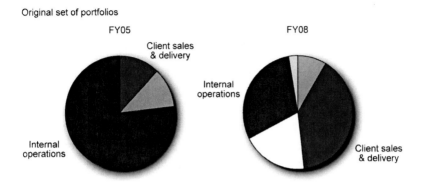

Figure 4: Changes in portfolio allocation

There is another important lesson to be learned here: do not expect to get IT governance correct straight out of the box. In my experience, a struggling IT function is often a sign that the IT governance model has not been well-defined, or that the people involved in the governance structures are not sufficiently experienced to make sound investment decisions. So take your best shot at a governance model, but then don't hesitate to make adjustments until the model faithfully reflects the intrinsic dynamics of your business.

Clarity around accountability

Whenever we talk about running IT like a business at Accenture, the value of two core business concepts shines through: stay close to your customers, and hold yourself and everyone around you accountable for results. The IT governance model I have outlined strives to put internal customers right next to IT professionals on the IT steering committee, so that the needs and priorities of your market-facing colleagues become IT's needs and priorities. Similarly, ensuring individuals' accountability for results is crucial both for long-term IT strategy and for day-to-day IT governance. The project champions and executive sponsors who propose a business case for change need to be there and be accountable when the benefits of that investment are calculated. We will return to the subject of accountability repeatedly in the chapters to come. Nothing can be more central to a business-like IT function than strict, rigorous accountability for results.

Running IT like a business

The technology is the easy part

We opened this chapter with the topic of IT strategy, before turning to the subject of IT governance. In the real world, you simply do not get the chance to handle the strategy part first, and then turn your attention to governance. What makes managing IT so challenging is that you have to get both the strategy process and the governance structures working simultaneously, and with a high degree of synchronization, if you want to function at a high level. So it is hardly an overstatement to say that the technology is the easy part of IT. Far more complex and nuanced are the strategic considerations and interpersonal relationships that must be managed whenever smart people come together to collaborate on a common task. IT strategy and IT governance are the foundational building blocks for high-performance IT. Master these competencies, and you will have made an excellent start on your journey toward IT transformation.

CHAPTER 2: CRAFTING A MENU OF MANAGED SERVICES

You have immersed yourself in the strategic goals of your enterprise. You and your colleagues have defined and aligned your IT strategy to support those larger goals. After considerable effort, you have also constructed a workable structure for IT governance. So all that remains before you can begin running IT like a business is to hang up a sign outside the entrance to the IT function that reads, "Open for Business."

Not so fast. When your first customer walks through the door, picks up the phone, or more likely sends you an e-mail, what exactly are you going to sell them?

We have traced the processes needed to engage internal customers in a dialogue that will help the IT function understand their needs. The next logical step in building a customer-focused IT business is to actually give your internal customers a say in deciding which IT services they use, as well as how much they are willing to pay for those services.

Crafting a menu of managed services goes beyond the conventional concept of a charge-back model for IT. This is not simply about recapturing costs or making a profit. This is about carefully considering all the wants and needs your customers have shared with you, and then designing a rich, attractive and flexible menu of IT services and capabilities that meets those needs at market-competitive costs. It is easy to confuse the decision to go with a managed-services approach with the decision to recover some of the cost of providing such services. These decisions need to be made independently of one another. A managed-services approach defines the product or service you offer. A charge-back plan defines how your economic model is going to work.

Your managed services menu should allow every customer to find what they need at the service levels and price points they feel are fair for their business units. Your menu will reflect your clear understanding of where costs are being generated and allocated; cost transparency is vital when dealing with what is essentially a captive customer base. In most large-scale corporate settings, internal customers do not have the option of shopping around for a better deal. The IT function must be prepared to hold itself accountable for the product and service commitments spelled out in the menu. Above all, your menu should make it easy for your customers to work with the IT function, since that is the primary purpose of having a menu in the first place.

After itemizing all the attributes of a successful menu, it soon becomes clear how complex the process of crafting that menu will become. What's more, you are unlikely to get the menu exactly right the first time. Like any business, you will discover, over time, which items are popular, which are not, and which are missing – because customers will tell you. So you will tweak here, add there, make a hundred and one minor adjustments, and gradually construct offerings that leave your customers satisfied that they are receiving the IT services they need, and that they are getting real value for their money.

For many IT functions, putting IT decisions in the hands of the business – which is the essence of managed services – represents a radical departure from traditional approaches to IT provisioning. Instead of IT dictating which services will be made available, internal customers get to decide what is best for their business units. Beginning to define IT in terms that will resonate with your customers demands a categorical shift in thinking. You are no longer in charge of IT. The customer is the boss.

Standards and specials

Each IT organization will have its own unique menu of products and services with different service levels, different service level guarantees, and different price points. To illustrate the menu of managed services supported by Accenture, *see Figure 5*. This is not offered as a model or a recommendation, but simply as one way of constructing a standard lineup of products and services:

Communications	Unified communications and collaboration
• Network connectivity • Remote access • Arranged services – communications	• Unified messaging (including e-mail) • Collaboration • Team services • File services • Telephony • Conferencing and streaming • Mobile device services • Identity and access services • Arranged services – unified communications and collaboration
Technical support • Self service (eSupport) • Service desk • Local support • Arranged services – tech support	
Hosting • Data center hosting – physical • Data center hosting – virtual • Local server room hosting	**Business applications** • Consulting • Outsourcing • Business process outsourcing • Pricing • Sales • Geographic services • Finance • HR • Corporate services • Local applications
Workstation • Hardware • Software • Services • Print services • Arranged services – workstation	**Publishing services** • Managed portal channels • Publishing sites

Figure 5: Accenture IT products and services 2011 catalog

The Accenture menu groups products and services in seven broad categories:

1. **Communications:** This category covers standard communications capabilities, including network connectivity and remote access. It also includes special arranged services. An example of arranged services would be the communications services and support

required by a large-scale meeting at an off-site location, such as a hotel.

2. **Technical support:** This category includes technical support in all its manifestations, ranging from self-service or eSupport to call-in service desk functions and in-person technical support. Once again, the category provides for arranged services provided under special circumstances or conditions, with terms of service and costs negotiated on a custom basis.

3. **Hosting:** The hosting category covers both physical and virtual hosting at Accenture data centers, as well as hosting services at local Accenture sites and offices.

4. **Workstations:** This category encompasses physical workstations – whether desktop or portable laptop computers – and includes hardware equipment and maintenance, desktop configuration, software provisioning and print services, as well as arranged services.

5. **Unified communications and collaboration:** This already large and steadily growing category includes e-mail provisioning, instant messaging and many other channels for collaboration. Tools include unified communications solutions, team services – such as SharePoint® – file services, telephony, audio and videoconferencing solutions, support for mobile devices – such as smart phones – and identity and access management.

6. **Business applications:** This category includes off-the-shelf as well as custom business applications programs required by Accenture business units – these in the three major areas of consulting, technology and outsourcing,

and being in different geographic regions and different corporate functions, such as human resources and finance. Accenture's IT function supports approximately 525 global and local applications in total.

7. **Publishing services:** This category covers company-wide portals, business unit portals and publishing sites.

The category of "business applications" provides a good illustration of how Accenture's menu of managed service offerings has evolved over time. We originally approached these applications in the same way we approach applications development and maintenance for Accenture's business clients. Applications were labeled as "services", such as "plan and analyze", "design and build", and "run or operate". This approach did not resonate with our internal business customers, who tended to think of these applications as standalone products, rather than as sets of IT services. Business sponsors within Accenture would come to us, wondering how much it would cost to create and operate an application to support recruiting, personnel scheduling, or some other business task or process. So we shifted our orientation, and now approach each global and local application as a specific product, instead of as a set of services.

Case study number 1: e-mail

What happens when you start looking at the work being done by your IT function through the prism of managed services? The best way to illustrate the effects of a managed-services approach is to examine specific instances. Take e-mail as one example. It is hard to think about a more commoditized offering than e-mail, yet thinking about e-mail and mailbox sizes in terms of a product rather than a provision can yield surprising results.

Like many corporations and organizations, Accenture had a problem with e-mail back in the middle of the last decade. The problem was clear-cut: no one ever threw anything away. We saved everything that came into our inboxes – the good, the bad, the irrelevant and the extraneous, as well as all the attachments, whether those files were redundant, works in progress, or copies of copies. The reason we never threw out anything was because there was no cost associated with saving everything. Except that there was indeed a cost – a very sizable one – because Accenture's data storage requirements were rising year after year at astronomical rates, requiring us to purchase more servers and build more data centers to store all the servers. In this respect, our experience was exactly like the experience of many other enterprises – a situation that frequently prevails even today.

About six years ago, our managed-services mindset compelled us to begin addressing the issue. We first sat down with our geographic services unit leads – the people responsible for personal enablement technology – and said to them, "We would like to work with you to define a set of e-mail offerings. We will let you choose the product that works best for your people and business. Then, we are going to charge you for the mailbox size you actually need, based on our cost." We worked together to define a logical set of e-mail offerings, and arrived at the following service levels:

- Platinum: full functionality with a 600MB size limit on the mailbox

- Gold: full functionality with a 300MB size limit on the mailbox
- Silver: full functionality with a 150MB size limit on the mailbox
- Bronze: full functionality with a 50MB size limit on the mailbox
- E-mail forward: limited functionality.

Each offering in this set had a cost associated with it, and each of our customers could select the level of service their teams required.

Our internal customers loved the new scheme, because they were getting the ability to choose the product that best matched their business requirements. Everyone in the IT function liked it as well, because we were not dictating solutions, but letting the customer choose the best product for them.

In short order, in fact within one year, the average demand for mailbox storage at Accenture was cut nearly in half – from 275MB per person to 140MB per person. No one issued any mandate or dictum, and customer satisfaction remained high, yet we had significantly reduced the annual rate of growth in our data storage.

Case study number 2: technology support

Another real-world experience with technology support confirms the virtues of a managed-services approach. Again, Accenture along with many other companies faced the rising cost of providing desk-side, face-to-face technology support. At one time, this had been the standard way in which tech support was delivered, but the rising expense pushed us and many other IT shops to explore alternatives.

We knew that it cost Accenture about US$75 per incident resolved for in-person support, as compared with US$25 to resolve an incident via a service desk, and US$5-6 for self-service or eSupport. With such compelling cost differentials, we began to structure a menu of services for technology support. All three modes of support – self-service, service desk/help desk support and local desk-side support – would always be available, but we used the cost-per-incident data to educate our colleagues on the cost differential, and we charged each business unit for the level of service selected.

In the case of technology support, the results of the managed-services approach were even more dramatic than in the e-mail example given earlier. Figure 6 shows how the introduction of managed services shifted the use of technology support away from service desk and local desk-side support to eSupport. In 2001, eSupport had not yet been introduced, so service desk support and local desk-side support accounted for 100% of the first point of contact for help. By 2011, local desk-side support had decreased to only one in ten incidents, and service desk calls accounted for less than one third of cases. Fully 60% of technology support was being provided via self-service eSupport, because it was dramatically cheaper and more popular with our customers. eSupport is available on the customer's terms – anytime and anywhere.

Results:
* Use cost per incident to educate the business
* First point of contact for help:

	2001	2007	2011
eSupport	NA	40%	60%
Service desk	65%	40%	30%
Local desk-side support	35%	20%	10%

Figure 6: Managed services technology support

Figure 6 illustrates how dramatically the IT function can change customer behavior through the introduction of managed services offerings.

Figure 7 shows how we worked to improve the delivery of technology services over a six-year period from FY 2002 through FY 2007. Managed services were one of the important innovations made during this period, as shown in FY 2003. By focusing on a given service as a product that can be developed and enhanced, the managed-service mindset leads naturally to incremental improvement over time. But the introduction of a managed-services approach was not the only change, and not even the most significant change. Only through the accumulation of many significant improvements in the delivery of technology support were we able to reduce the cost per headcount to US$272 in FY 2007 from US$665 in FY 2002.

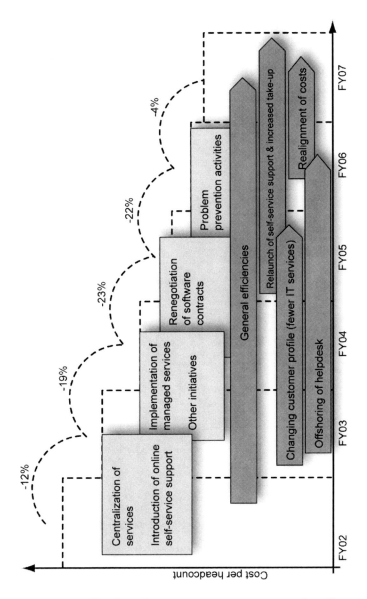

Figure 7: Technology support cost reduction

Think product and service

When you begin thinking about products and services in IT, you take another step away from the provisioning of services and toward running IT like a business. Analyzing your products and services creates the opportunity to ask fundamental questions about your work *(see Figure 8).*

	Technology support	Desktop management and mobility	Business applications
Demand management • Customer segmentation • Tailored service levels and costs • Affordable service levels.	• Shift from local support to help desk and eSupport • Reduced local support during standard office hours • Move to dispatch model for local support.	**How do we manage demand?**	
Productivity / performance management • Continuous improvement • New delivery models • IT infrastructure initiatives • Implementation of discretionary / non-resource pools.	• Problem prevention • Re-launch of eSupport • Application defect reporting and root cause analysis.	**How do we manage our productivity?**	
Supply management • Strategic sourcing • Service agreements with infrastructure outsourcing (IO), delivery centers, solutions workforce, Avanade.	• IO Accenture unit • Transition of help desk support to low-cost locations.	**How do we manage supply?**	

Figure 8: Improving managed services

How do we manage the demand for the product? In the case of technology support, what techniques would help us shift demand from local support to help desk and eSupport? These questions may lead you to consider restricting standard office hours for local support, or to move to a dispatch model for local support.

How can we manage our productivity? What can we do to eliminate the need for the help desk call in the first place? Can a concentrated focus on problem prevention help? Should we be doing more in the way of application defect reporting or root cause analysis? In the case of Accenture's technology support, we felt that eSupport did not have the necessary visibility and uptake, so we re-launched it in order to draw attention to the capability and its benefits – one of which was a lower cost.

How do we manage product supply? If we are selling help, where can we get more technical help at lower rates? At Accenture, these questions prompted us to begin outsourcing our help desk support to lower-cost offshore locations.

Think pricing

Central to any managed-services approach is the customer's willingness to pay for the service selected. Do you charge for every single IT activity? How do you determine market-competitive pricing? As soon as corporate budgets come into play, a number of potentially contentious issues arise. So let's establish pricing principles first.

We are not in the IT business to make money. In my view, the IT function exists to help the enterprise achieve its goals, not to become a profit center. So the goal should be to price as close to actual cost as possible. Whenever I have deviated from that principle, it has been at my peril. Case in point: after we introduced the tiered e-mail service described earlier, we decided to encourage internal customers to choose the silver-level offering, which provided a 150MB mailbox. So we priced this option slightly lower than our cost. Our customers are smart, and we were too successful – the result being that many customers moved to the silver-level offering in order to save money, leaving us unable to recover our real costs for the service.

You should only seek to make chargebacks where they will encourage important or valuable changes in user behavior. Beware of becoming ensnared in fruitless charge-back debates that bring no value to the enterprise. If your pricing exercise becomes a fight over bits and bytes in a misguided effort to charge back the value of your network, you need to reconsider your approach. At Accenture, our network is used globally by everyone; since we are going to manage products and their associated costs centrally, we do not charge the cost back to anyone.

The issue of whether or not you should be charging back for technology to support global business processes is another potentially difficult question. As a matter of principle, we at Accenture rule that if it is a global capability we will not charge for it. Your enterprise may make a different arrangement based on your IT function and the needs of your business.

Lastly, taking the managed services path commits you to being as rigorous as you possibly can be in benchmarking the total cost of IT services. Your customers do not have the option of going elsewhere if they do not like your service. So you have to be able to prove that the products and services you are selling are fairly and competitively priced.

There are a variety of tools available for determining the going market rate of a given service. For starters, you need to track how your IT costs are generated. If you are moving to a managed-services approach for the first time, you are probably starting from a point where your financial tracking is by "natural expense" – which includes labor, depreciation, maintenance, and other standard costs. To effectively implement a managed-services approach, it is imperative to develop a capability to manage the IT business along four primary dimensions: the IT product and service, the customer, the IT organization structure, and the natural expense.

Industry analysts are excellent sources of benchmarking information; these firms regularly solicit this kind of data from all the major players in the IT marketplace.

The pricing exercise serves as a valuable business benefit, even if you are not charging back your costs to an internal customer. By going through the discipline of preparing a mock invoice, your IT function can analyze the value you are getting from a given application or solution versus the cost. By using a "total cost of ownership" calculation – which covers everything from hosting, maintenance and support, packaged software maintenance, calls to the help desk and any other relevant expenses – you can evaluate the cost and benefits of given solutions, then search for outliers or exceptionally expensive tools. You can then investigate why particular applications may be costing more than the business value they are creating. This can lead to decisions to retire or replace technology solutions with ones that are more cost-effective or that generate more business value.

At Accenture, we used the mock invoice approach to assess the value of one particular application used for global personnel scheduling. This particular application was not a favorite among users and was difficult to maintain. After a mock invoice exercise, we discovered that it was the third most expensive application in our entire portfolio, which included several hundred applications. Further investigation revealed that we were spending several million dollars annually to support it, including US$3 million in hosting costs alone.

In the next investment development cycle, we moved to develop a new custom-built Accenture application called "myScheduling". We built a new tool in nine months, with a global, scalable architecture and an improved user interface. By building a better tool from scratch, we were able to reduce the cost of the application by 50%, while reducing the time required to support Accenture users by 68% – a win-win for the business and for IT.

Think customer

A managed-services approach to IT will force IT professionals to rethink ingrained habits and change the way they have been doing things for their entire careers. Old habits die hard, but the change is more than worth the effort because managed services give you a pragmatic framework for assessing where your IT function is adding genuine value to your enterprise. Thinking about IT with your customers' needs in mind enables you to understand the products and services you offer today, and forecast what you will need to be offering two or three years from now. Once you have a projected destination, you can plot your journey.

But it all starts with a deep understanding of your internal customers. The universe of internal customers in every enterprise will vary, depending on your business, industry, global footprint, and many other factors. But it is essential for you to develop a clear conception of your customer types, so that you can structure your IT services to suit them. By way of illustration, the following figure depicts how we see and work with our customers inside Accenture.

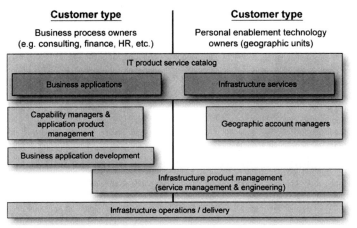

Figure 9: Working with your customers

Your managed services roadmap

Moving from a conventional provisioning of IT capabilities to a managed services business model is definitely a journey. How will you know you are making progress? Looking at our own journey, which began shortly after Accenture became a public company in 2001, we passed through four distinct phases in the evolution of our managed-services approach *(see Figure 10)*. If your experience mirrors ours, you will find your organization working its way through similar stages or phases.

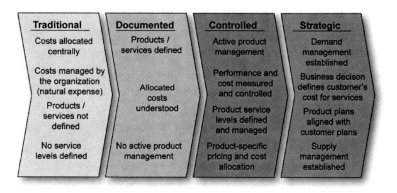

Traditional	Documented	Controlled	Strategic
Costs allocated centrally	Products / services defined	Active product management	Demand management established
Costs managed by the organization (natural expense)	Allocated costs understood	Performance and cost measured and controlled	Business decison defines customer's cost for services
Products / services not defined		Product service levels defined and managed	Product plans aligned with customer plans
No service levels defined	No active product management	Product-specific pricing and cost allocation	Supply management established

Figure 10: Managed services product roadmap

In the first, or "traditional," stage, costs are either allocated centrally or not at all, and are managed by the IT organization based on "natural expense" calculations. Products and services are not defined, and there are no service level commitments.

In the second phase, which could be called the "documented" stage, you will begin to master the basics of managed services: defining your core products and services, and building your understanding of how to estimate and calculate costs on a broad level. In this still-early part of the journey, you may not be quite ready for an active and aggressive approach to product management, but you will be beginning to think about IT products for the first time.

With the passage of time and the acquisition of valuable experience, you will then move into a "controlled" stage. Product managers are assigned specific responsibilities for a product portfolio. Performance metrics are established, and costs are being measured with increasing precision. In consultation with your internal customers, you will be defining product service levels and setting service level agreements. You will also begin negotiating product-specific pricing and cost allocations with those same customers, who will be beginning to gain a deeper appreciation of the value your IT function delivers to their business operations.

In the fourth, or "strategic," phase of the journey, your managed-services approach enables you to undertake high-level, strategic management of demand and supply. Your internal customers are choosing products less on cost and more on business need and value delivered. Through regular consultation and communication with internal customer groups, and through your established IT governance structures, you are continuously aligning your IT product catalog with the business plans of your customers, so that as their business changes, so does your product offering.

Running IT like a business

Prize well worth the pain

In my conversations with IT colleagues, many executives acknowledge that they have heard about managed services and are quite interested in giving this approach a try. But they consistently cite problems with implementation, and those problems invariably center on changing the culture of the IT organization itself. There is rarely a problem getting the senior leaders of the business or enterprise to buy the concept; generally, they love the idea. Internal customers are typically enthusiastic as well; after all, they are getting choices they never had before, so what's not to like? The serious problems emerge from within the ranks of IT itself.

Technologists are simply not used to thinking about IT in a business context. The vast majority of the IT shops I've had the opportunity to work with during my career tend to be technology-focused; a business orientation simply goes against the grain.

If you encounter this resistance, do not be discouraged. In fact, you can plan for it. We at Accenture ran into the same issues. When we began to explore managed services in a serious and disciplined way back in the early 2000s, several IT leaders were adamantly opposed. The honest truth is that we found it very hard to get take up and receptivity throughout the IT organization.

What turned things around was the demonstrated ability of managed services to take costs out of the IT operation. The dot.com bubble had just burst, and we were facing demands from Accenture's leadership to reduce costs dramatically in IT operations in very short periods of time. I can remember receiving what then seemed like weekly calls to find multi-million dollar reductions in IT costs. Before managed services, we had no framework for having a discussion with the business on what we should reduce. Managed services gave us the perfect construct and a very powerful framework for having a constructive conversation around cost reduction. So the prize is well worth the pain.

CHAPTER 3: TRACKING IT PERFORMANCE

Operations in today's IT department are typically measured against a wide variety of technical standards: network uptime, incidents logged and resolved, workstation failure rates, and so on. While this is an excellent start, these technical metrics are only the beginning of a comprehensive reporting framework. If your goal is to run your IT function like a business, then you need to track the performance of your function in the same ways that any business measures its performance. To make informed decisions as you manage the IT function, you need accurate information on what is working. To articulate IT performance to your enterprise leadership and to stakeholders, you must be able to translate technical metrics into credible measures of value creation. In this chapter, we will examine the tools and techniques of performance measurement.

Accurate metrics and reporting are invaluable in helping IT executives make good decisions. As managers, we need to know how the IT function is performing in order to know where to focus improvement efforts and new investments. Tracking IT performance is also critical for demonstrating the business value of your IT function; without such measures, it is difficult to communicate the value of your function, or to make a case for additional funding and investment.

The commitment you bring to performance measurement is critical for its success. Anyone can overlay a veneer of performance metrics on top of an existing operation, showing improvement year after year, and many do precisely that. It is another matter to measure your shop rigorously against the relevant benchmarks in your industry or sector, to be prepared to acknowledge shortcomings, and to commit your IT operation fully to a discipline of accountability.

So, in addition to examining performance measures, we will also explore how to gather and utilize benchmarking data that adds credibility to your internal performance measurements.

Performance measurements

There is no shortage of tracking and reporting data in IT operations. But how do you make sense of all the reporting you already have? How do you identify the additional tracking you should be doing? And how do you put everything into a framework that supports your goal of running IT like a business?

Each enterprise will answer these questions with its own uniquely engineered reporting system and structure. The reporting framework utilized in Accenture's IT organization takes the shape of a funnel, as depicted in Figure 11:

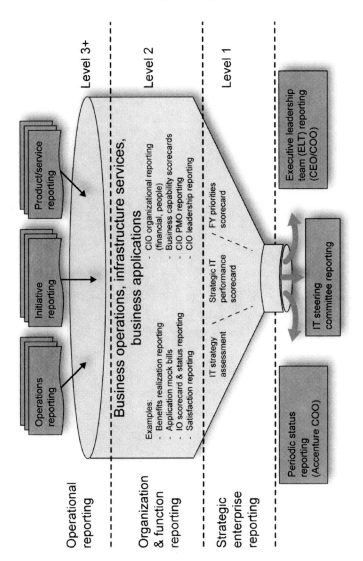

Figure 11: Accenture IT organization's reporting framework

Working from the top down, the lowest level – or operational Level 3+ – of reporting, includes project-level reporting on individual initiatives, status reporting, product and service reporting, and other reporting generated on a daily or weekly basis.

Data from this level is then rolled up into Level 2 organization and function reporting, grouped in the three major areas of Accenture's IT function: business operations, infrastructure services and business applications. Reports at this level synthesize data from multiple sources into more coherent portraits of the IT function's performance, and are typically produced on a monthly timetable.

Examples of Level 2 reports include:

- Benefits realization reporting
- Application mock bills/invoices
- Infrastructure operations scorecard and status reporting
- Satisfaction reporting
- CIO organizational reporting (financial, people)
- Business capability scorecards
- CIO project management office (PMO) reporting
- CIO leadership reporting.

Level 1 strategic enterprise reporting examines the IT function holistically and constitutes the highest level of abstraction and synthesis. Individual scorecards for IT strategy, IT performance and priorities in the current fiscal year track multiple metrics that are meaningful to the overall business. These reports are submitted to the IT steering committee and to Accenture's chief operating officer, and also inform reporting to Accenture's executive leadership team (ELT).

Figure 12 displays one of the Level 1 scorecards, which illustrates the level of detail and the metric tracked.

IT contribution	Sponsor satisfaction	% satisfied and very satisfied
	Employee satisfaction	% satisfied and very satisfied
	Critical processes / roles	% satisfied and very satisfied
	Benefits enabled (realized business case benefits) Collected in Q2	FY09 and FY10 (% realized, $ actual to date)
	Market image	Market and business development contributions
IT operational excellence	IT expense as % of net revenue	%
	IT expense per Accenture employee	$ per person
	Consulting workforce	$ per person
	Enterprise workforce	$ per person
	Services workforce	$ per person
	Solutions workforce	$ per person
	Business process outsourcing	$ per person
	IT productivity / cost effectiveness improvements	$ (Δ IT expense per employee headcount)
	Service levels	% targets achieved
	IT expense (with interest)	Quarter ending reforecast
	On-time delivery of FY10 initiatives	% delivered on time (collected in Q4)
	Workforce targets	Permanent workforce (#,%) Variable workforce (#,%) % US / % non-US
	IT workforce, with Infrastructure Outsourcing Accenture unit, as % of Accenture headcount	%
Best in class workplace	Overall employee attrition – unmanaged / managed	%
	Executives – unmanaged / managed	%
	Non-executives – unmanaged / managed	%
	Employee attrition – top performers, unmanaged	%
	Employee satisfaction	Satisfaction index %
	% of training budget spent	%

Figure 12: Strategic IT performance scorecard (sample)

This sample scorecard brings together metrics in three key areas:

1. The contribution IT is making to the success of the business, as measured in:

   - Satisfaction among business sponsors, employees and critical processes/roles
   - Benefits enabled or realized business case benefits
   - Market image, or IT's contribution to Accenture's new business development effort.

2. IT operational excellence, as measured by:

   - IT cost as percentage of net revenue
   - IT expense per employee – overall and by distinct workforce
   - Improvements in productivity, service levels, delivery and other targets.

3. Measures of Accenture's IT function as a best-in-class workplace, as seen in:

   - Employee attrition
   - Employee satisfaction
   - Percent of training budget spent.

Accenture's reporting structure for its IT organization balances considerable detail with strategic synthesis. But we did not start out here. We developed the levels of reporting depicted here over a two-year period, then refined and adjusted the metrics for several more years before arriving at the current framework. Its maturity is evident in the fact that it has remained fairly stable over the last six years.

Given that Accenture is a highly centralized enterprise, we found it comparatively easy to assemble this framework, and to ensure that its scorecards are aligned with overall IT strategy and governance. The reporting structure for a decentralized or federated enterprise would, undoubtedly, look quite different. In a distributed enterprise, the key metrics at the centralized or federated level may be primarily financial in nature, while divisional measures would focus on service and satisfaction levels. If your enterprise is a holding company and its subsidiaries operate in different sectors or markets, consolidating lower-level measures to the corporate level may be less informative. You will want to avoid rolling up operational metrics wherever this tends to obscure meaningful distinctions. For example, if your enterprise operates manufacturing businesses and financial services units, IT spending as a percentage of net revenue may be in the 1-2% range for the former, and in the 7-10% range for the latter. To combine comparable metrics from such dissimilar IT operations would serve little purpose.

Allowing for such variances, many of the metrics used by Accenture can be applied to any IT operation. Having worked with many government agencies at the local, state and national levels, as well as with non-profit organizations, I can attest to the utility of these metrics in those enterprises. All IT organizations exist to serve their businesses, and all are delivering the same basic services. So while there may be some differences in levels of benchmarks from sector to sector – such as the difference between manufacturing and financial services – it is still important to understand what you are doing and to understand upward and downward trends.

As you assemble the reporting framework suited to your enterprise, the important lesson to keep in mind is that you should not expect to get it perfect right away. Many companies seek to be too good, and waste valuable time and energy debating nuances, when only time and experience will reveal the right metric or structure for your enterprise.

Measuring satisfaction

Collecting data for performance measurement is normally a clear-cut process of quantification, until you come to measures of user satisfaction. Asking customers, "How are we doing?" can be eye-opening, jaw-dropping or mind-boggling, depending on your performance and the user providing the response. Despite the variable nature of the outcome, this interrogation is essential, so much so that at Accenture we actively solicit customer opinions on our performance. Not being afraid to ask your customers what they think of you is an indispensable part of running IT like a business.

At Accenture, we divide the customer universe into two broad groups: sponsors, or those that hire IT and purchase our services, and users or employees – those who actually use our services to do their jobs.

For sponsor satisfaction surveys, we further divide this group into business process sponsors, who buy applications and infrastructure services from IT, and geographic sponsors – the executives responsible for all of Accenture's business activities in specified geographic areas. All business and geographic sponsors are surveyed annually on the quality of IT services they are receiving and their perceptions of IT's overall performance, including measures of reliability, cost effectiveness and business value.

With business process sponsors, our survey instrument is ourselves. Executives from Accenture's CIO Organization personally interview several functional leads in each major unit every quarter. In face-to-face conversations, we engage in a dialogue, hearing feedback firsthand, responding on a real-time basis, and building personal relationships along the way.

The advantage of in-person interaction is obvious, but it is not always practical; therefore, with geographic sponsors, we rely on surveys to minimize time and travel costs.

When it comes to gathering responses from those Accenture employees who are our end users, we actually survey one twelfth of our end-user universe each month. In effect, we survey every line employee in Accenture once a year, every year. These surveys do not elicit 100% response rates, but this blanket approach to the user base ensures a continuous stream of user feedback.

When we first began conducting these surveys, our IT product managers and directors tended to regard the survey as a nuisance. Our persistence has turned around that attitude completely; IT employees now clamor for the opportunity to receive direct feedback on issues and concerns in technology. We devote a considerable amount of effort to refining the questions that are being asked, and in reviewing the answers and comments that come in, reading between the lines for the product and service insights that only customers can provide. Just as if we were running a global food franchise and saw a sudden drop-off in same-store sales in a particular locality, rising numbers of technology complaints from a particular region signal a trouble that needs to be addressed immediately. The fact that we conduct the user survey on a rolling monthly schedule helps us spot changing business requirements or service delivery issues early, and respond quickly.

Metric management

The metrics you collect on your IT performance will enable you to track operations over time and determine whether your team is making progress and, if so, how much. As with any data-gathering process, consistency of methodology over time is essential to ensure meaningful comparisons.

Another important facet of what might be termed metric management is retaining your ability to drill down through the data you gather, so that you can begin to answer the question of what is happening, and why.

Figure 13 illustrates the scorecard we use to track our performance at Accenture around the specific area of core IT architecture – which includes network connectivity, remote access, data center hosting and application monitoring. We use a typical red/yellow/green classification of results to aid with visual assessment of data. As you begin to collect data like this on your own operation, and then roll it up into higher-level reporting to senior management, it is vital to retain the ability to drill down from the highest level back to the operational level, so that you can effectively diagnose the reasons why your results may be varying from your targets.

Network connectivity	Metric	Feb '10	Mar '10	Apr '10	May '10	Variance	Targets	End of FY10
Overall	# of devices managed	5,882	5,952	5,861	5,724			
	Network connectivity cost per headcount	$529	$528	$505	$500	$17	≤ $482	
LAN	Customer satisfaction – wired	92.3%	92.6%	93.3%	95.2%	2.3%	≥ 92.9%	
	Customer satisfaction – wireless	84.9%	85.7%	85.6%	87.5%			
	# of wired points	92,914	92,242	92,242	92,242			
	# of wireless access points	1,454	1,520	1,519	1,587			
	LAN availability	99.97%	99.93%	99.99%	99.97%	0.07%	≥ 99.90%	
WAN	# of MB³ managed	16,767	14,993	14,993	14,623			
	Global WAN availability	100%	99.99%	100%	99.99%	0.00%	≥ 99.90%	
	Cost per MB (monthly)	$578	$578	$579			≤ $675	

Remote access	Metric	Feb '10	Mar '10	Apr '10	May '10	Variance	Targets	End of FY10
Overall	Customer satisfaction	88.1%	90.4%	87.3%	90.3%	-1.7%	≥ 92%	
	% of successful connection attempts	88.2%	87.6%	88.1%	86.8%	1.8%	≥ 85%	
	# of extended service users subscribed	6,936	6,890	6,908	7,083	83	≥ 7,000	
Extended services	# of Wi-fi hours	13,391	15,776	13,075	13,403			
	% of users exceeding 25 hrs/month	1.3%	1.8%	1.4%	1.3%	-3.7%	≤ 5.0%	
	Average cost per extended service user	$15.70	$16.42	$14.64	$14.50	-$0.50	≤ $15.00	

³ megabytes

Data center hosting	Metric	Feb '10	Mar '10	Apr '10	May '10	Variance	Targets	End of FY10
Overall	Customer satisfaction	87.7%	93%	97.3%	92.2%	2.2%	≥ 90.0%	
	Hosting cost versus forecast	102.5%	102.2%	103.7%	104.3%	4.3%	≥ 100%	
Physical	# of machines	1,422	1,376	1,327	1,258			
	Platform availability	Metric not yet available						
Virtual	# of machines	1,556	1,628	1,687	1,737			
	Average utilization of VMs[4]	70.3%	73.3%	73.3%	73.3%	-1.7%	75.0%	
	Platform availability	Metric not yet available						
Storage	# of TB[5]	1,007	1,056	990	1,067			
	% of storage used	Metric not yet available						
Local server room	# of locally hosted servers	1,434	1,394	1,392	1,315			

Application monitoring	Metric	Feb '10	Mar '10	Apr '10	May '10	Variance	Targets	End of FY10
	Critical application availability	99.99%	99.59%	99.97%	99.81%	0.81%	≥ 99%	

Monitoring tools	Metric	Feb '10	Mar '10	Apr '10	May '10	Variance	Targets	End of FY10
	Systems management incidents	1,959	2,547	1,953	1,896			
	Total automated incidents	23,367	23,347	19,445	17,636			
	Total automated incidents including "systems management"	25,326	25,894	21,398	19,532			

Figure 13: Core architecture scorecard (sample)

[4] virtual machines
[5] terabytes

Another important dimension of data gathering concerns differences in the data across geographies. Managers of global enterprises know how costs for applications and labor can vary from location to location. So your metric management should include the capability of analyzing data on a geographic basis, as well as on the other relevant parameters of your enterprise.

To illustrate the implications of data-gathering on a global scale, Figure 14 depicts the way we look at Accenture's businesses along three dimensions: by geography, by operating groups, and by our major growth platforms, with corporate functions underpinning all these operations.

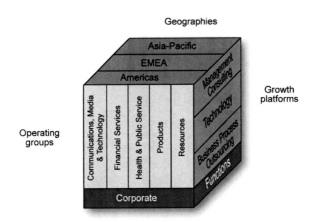

Figure 14: Accenture's organizational structure

This structure is used to guide many of the metrics we gather on IT operations, so that we can report on IT performance in the corporate aggregate, and also drill down to report on IT performance at lower levels of the enterprise. The ability to look at metrics with detail and precision will help you identify outliers – those products or services you offer that may be costing your operation significantly more than the norm.

For instance, we all understand that many IT products and services have a local labor component, and that the costs for these can vary widely. The cost for local in-person support in the US is typically several times as much as the same level of support in a country such as India. So you will want to be able to isolate and identify those cost components. This level of detail in your metrics will also enable you to compare costs from region to region. "Why is our IT support in the US costing so much more than support costs in the UK?" is just one example of the kinds of useful questions that will lead to illuminating discussions as you review your metrics within the IT organization and with the senior leadership of your organization.

Benchmarking

Metrics create the first half of the case you make to corporate or organizational leadership that you are running an effective and successful IT operation. Benchmarking against relevant industry and IT standards provides the other half of the value equation.

With benchmarking, you can make the case that you are measuring your operation with rigorous methods, and that your performance compares favorably with the operations of comparable IT functions in other companies, or with prevailing standards in the IT marketplace.

Without benchmarking, your argument carries little weight. You may be able to demonstrate that your operational performance has improved over last year's results, but such improvements merely beg the question, "As compared to what?"

Benchmarking lends credence to the performance measurements you present to senior management, and lends credibility to the value proposition you make to each one of your internal customers. Benchmarking is so central to what we do at Accenture, that we conduct this process on two distinct levels.

First, we use major metrics to benchmark our work against our competitors – which are other IT service firms with annual revenues in excess of US$6 billion. We measure three variables:

- IT costs as a percentage of net revenue
- IT costs per person supported
- IT workforce as a percentage of total workforce.

We retain an independent industry-consulting specialist to conduct a custom IT benchmark survey for Accenture, comparing these three metrics across companies and industry sectors. Industry analysts have access to IT cost information by industry, so it is far more feasible to commission these surveys than to attempt to conduct them directly ourselves.

Accenture also conducts product- and service-level benchmarking, which is the second level of comparative measurement. We examine many individual IT components, such as e-mail provisioning and help desk service, seeking to determine if our costs – as identified through internal metrics – are competitive with those of other companies in our field. If not, we seek to learn why not, and what must be done to correct a negative cost differential.

What do we expect to learn from the benchmarking of all our services? Sometimes, we learn very little, particularly when the product or service is mature and there are few opportunities for performance improvement. In other circumstances, we may discover that while our service has not changed, the marketplace has – a discovery that forces us to reconsider how we are providing a given service.

For example, as a result of Accenture's annual benchmarking exercise, we noticed that the typical industry costs for a commodity-type service were declining fairly rapidly. Upon further investigation, we determined that several technological innovations were combining to make the outsourcing of this service feasible. Even though the metrics over the past several years indicated that we were doing a good job on this service, we had to recognize that we would not be able to compete as the cost prevailing in the marketplace continued to fall. So we are actively exploring the outsourcing of a central service not because we changed, but because the world did.

As with any metric, it is imperative to establish consistent definitions for what you are measuring and a consistent way of developing the benchmark you want to use. While you can never be absolutely certain that you are getting an "apples-to-apples" comparison, you cannot argue with data trends that hold over several years.

When Accenture began its IT performance measurement program in earnest back in 2001, we focused on the three metrics cited above, and we maintained this focus year after year. Today, we can see in Figure 15 the fruits of these labors in the significant declines our IT transformation has been able to achieve for Accenture.

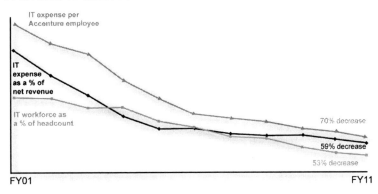

Figure 15: Major Accenture IT metrics, 2001-2010

Even more instructive are the benchmarking results that compare our performance on these three metrics against results from comparable companies. These results give us the ability to state, with a high degree of confidence, that Accenture's IT organization performs at levels equal to the lowest metrics or substantially below the lowest metrics recorded in our industry.

Benefits realization

Even after you have completed your performance measurements and your annual benchmarking exercise, something more remains to be done. Inside Accenture, we describe this with the innocuous term of "benefits realization." In reality, the processes of IT performance measurement and value creation remain incomplete until all the processes discussed in this chapter are linked back to the investment decisions made through the IT governance structure first discussed in Chapter 1.

Figure 16: Life cycle of IT investment benefits realization

Figure 16 illustrates a full life cycle view of IT investments. It is instructive to trace the four stages of the life cycle in order to understand the importance of benefits realization when running IT like a business.

Recalling our original discussion of IT governance, we noted that, as part of any decision to proceed with IT investments, it is necessary to create a business case for the investment and to establish the baseline benefits the investment is expected to deliver. This business case with its associated benefits is then reviewed with the IT steering committee before investment commitments are finalized.

After an investment decision is taken and a business case approved, we track that investment for three years beyond implementation, in order to determine whether or not we are achieving the benefits promised by the business case. The return on Accenture's IT investment is measured with rigor to determine the actual benefits realized in relation to the original business case. The results of this performance tracking are then fed back into the investment planning process, in order to inform future decision making based on actual results.

It is vital to note that only benefits that can be fully documented are considered "realized." In the early years of our own governance process, we discerned a tendency toward what might be called "fiction writing" when it came to documenting the business cases achieved. To counteract that natural tendency, Accenture assigns its own internal audit group, which is wholly independent of the IT function. Internal Audit conducts audits of a selected random sample of business cases, including physical visits to locations and the examination of documented evidence of benefits achieved. If the objective evidence of the benefit is not confirmed during the audit, the business sponsor who stands accountable for the realization of the business case gets no credit for it. As an additional safeguard against degradation of benefits targets, any revisions to the benefits to be achieved require the approval of the IT steering committee.

Running IT like a business

No one is perfect, and that's perfectly OK

The issue at the center of performance measurement is the very human reality of imperfection. In IT, as in life, no one likes to acknowledge anything less than perfection. We are quite happy to admit our limitations on a conceptual level, but how many of us are enthusiastic when it comes to measuring the precise extent of our imperfections, year after year? Yet performance measurements and benchmarking commits us not simply to the measurement of our limitations, but to an obsession with them. In running IT like a business, we are committing ourselves and our organizations to a process of continuous improvement that never ends. The upside of imperfection is that it is precisely through the acknowledgment of shortcomings that we open the doors to improvement. So no IT operation is perfect, and that is precisely the way it is supposed to be. The good news is that the field in which we work – information technology – is one where continuous improvement is not only possible, but demonstrably doable. When Moore's Law was first postulated in 1965, how many truly believed that it would hold true for more than five decades, without interruption? The beauty of IT as a field of endeavor is that incremental but cumulatively dramatic reductions in operating costs, as well as gains in reliability and value creation, are well within the grasp of every IT operation – as we will continue to discover in the next chapter.

CHAPTER 4: CREATING VALUE ACROSS THE ENTERPRISE

We have explored several related dimensions of what it means to run IT like a business. Beginning with IT strategy and governance, we looked at the necessary foundations for a business-like approach to IT. A look into the managed-services mindset helped us to begin thinking about our internal customers and their needs. We saw that performance measurements supply a source of credible information and a vital measure of accountability.

All these activities are necessary in themselves, but something more is required in order for your IT function to complete its transformation from cost center into value center. We have reached that point in a transformational journey where our basic operations are effective, we are meeting the needs of our customers, and we are measuring our performance. We are now ready to go beyond meeting the specific requirements of internal clients, and begin searching for opportunities to add value to the wider enterprise.

This pursuit of higher-level value creation initiatives enables the IT function to become a true strategic partner for the enterprise by solving problems and creating solutions that extend well beyond the function's menu of managed services.

In this chapter, we will explore the many avenues of value creation open to the IT function. We will also discuss how to communicate the value once you have created it. I believe that every corporate function, and particularly IT, needs to be absolutely clear in communicating the value they provide to their corporation, their organization, or their government department. If we are not clear about the value that IT delivers, how can we expect executive leadership to estimate our value accurately, or to continue to allocate the investments required to keep our IT business healthy? If other people in the enterprise are not clear, they will eventually wonder whether the function should even exist. So communicating the value created is, in a very practical sense, as important as the value itself.

Let's begin by examining the surprising number of ways in which IT can create value for the enterprise. Even though not every option discussed here will be appropriate or relevant for every organization, what is important is for you to begin looking for and taking advantage of the opportunities available to your IT function in your organizational setting.

Doing more for less

Ask yourself and your IT colleagues this simple question: how can we do what we do better, faster and cheaper next year than we did last year?

Many IT executives might consider such a question suicidal. "Why try doing things cheaper? We should be asking for budget increases, not reductions." Given the astonishing power of IT, such a question is not dangerous, but entirely doable, and not just this year, but year after year.

To note that many IT people do not share this mindset is not an indictment, but an honest recognition that people go into IT because they are technologists before they are business people. Technical capability is always going to be more important to a technologist than operating efficiency. But our experience at Accenture demonstrates that, when you focus on value creation, you actually can have both the best technology and the most efficient technology operation. In fact, excellent technology fuels efficient technology, and vice versa. By taking advantage of new technology developments, you accelerate the process of change, and so are able to provide things better, faster and cheaper than you ever considered possible.

The examples of this are so plentiful that we need cite only a few obvious cases. Consider how network bandwidth has changed over the past 10 years alone, turning videoconferencing from an executive-level luxury into a staff-level commonplace. Who imagined in the year 2000 that we would be running enterprise-wide applications on our cell phones? SharePoint® capabilities in many enterprises now allow a virtual team, collaborating across great distances and many time zones, to acquire a shared internal workspace, populate it, and start using it in minutes – all without intervention or support from IT. How about the explosion in sourcing and alternative delivery methods? Every year there is something so new and so innovative that you are forced to wonder where it will all end. But it never does end, as the cycle of innovation keeps renewing itself.

Technology professionals love the "next new thing", but we also have to live with our stable-state predisposition, in which change is the great unspoken threat. Injecting change increases risk, and the last thing in the world we as IT professionals want to see is downtime or systemic problems initiated by our own changes. Nevertheless, change we must, because not wanting to change and failing to adapt will itself cause changes, even in the short term. The minute you stop changing, you are losing ground, if for no other reason than because competitors are making changes all the time.

So where should you look inside your function if you want to do things better, faster and cheaper? Here are eight separate areas you may want to explore:

Centralize, standardize, consolidate: Many IT professionals believe that they need best-of-breed solutions in each major area of operations. Our experience shows that, while the best-of-breed philosophy is at first attractive, it imposes complexity and reduces flexibility over time. This is why we strive for the Theme of One in every area of IT operations. Less is always more, and one is always preferred. Accenture's entire enterprise operates on a single global platform, from desktop through data center. We may make minor sacrifices in capability and performance here and there, but we gain in many other ways, simplifying everything.

Smart sourcing: Are you taking advantage of all the available sources and your lowest-cost resources for your technology force? Despite our world-class in-house technology team, Accenture's internal IT function actually outsources significant blocks of our operation . . . to other parts of Accenture! In a global team of approximately 4,000 IT professionals, slightly less than 500 are part of the formal CIO Organization; the rest come from various other parts of the company. Some 2,000 professionals are drawn from Accenture's Global Delivery Network. Virtually all our infrastructure operations are outsourced to the Accenture Infrastructure Outsourcing Unit. At any given point in time, several hundred other professionals are seconded from Accenture's consulting practice. With variable resources making up as much as 85% of our global

IT team, we can ramp up or down as workloads fluctuate, without sacrificing 24/7 coverage.

Rationalize applications: Proliferation of applications afflicts every enterprise these days, so Accenture's experience may be instructive. The process of rationalizing applications is no more glamorous than unstacking bricks: eliminate redundant applications, drop applications that are near the end of their useful lives and, wherever possible, drive applications to standardized architectures and platforms. Reducing the number of applications simplifies the environment, enabling lower costs and greater speed in delivering new capabilities. A hidden benefit of application rationalization is that the enterprise, in many situations, will regain a single source of the truth, as opposed to having multiple applications with different data. The result is better decision making all around.

Consolidate and virtualize data centers: Your data center operations could become a gold mine for better, faster and cheaper improvements. In 2001, Accenture data centers were spread across as many as 40 locations worldwide. Today, five data centers with half the space are saving the company 60% of 2001 costs. New server, database and storage software technologies are now turning the consolidation effort into a full-scale virtualization project. As thin provisioning and other techniques allow multiple applications and databases to use shared hardware, the days of having one server for each application are history. More than 80% of Accenture data centers are already virtualized, and this number continues to climb.

Transform your network: Driven by new technology capabilities and the opportunity to reduce costs, Accenture completely redid its global communications network. The change, including implementation of MPLS across the network enabled data and voice traffic to flow through the same channels, reducing costs by approximately 20%, or US$25 million annually. Equally significant, the revamped network enabled a spectrum of new collaboration technologies and tools, including one of the world's largest high-definition videoconferencing networks.

Re-engineer processes: This type of re-engineering can be as basic as rebuilding a global print capability, so that any professional in your enterprise can print a document on any printer in the world with just a few clicks. It could be as expansive as re-engineering the entire technology support function to create self-support capabilities. When we made the switch to self-service IT support, we found that we could handle more than 65% of all incidents at a cost of less than 10% of a physical visit.

Consolidate suppliers and contracts: It is basic business sense to seek, wherever possible, to consolidate contracts with multiple suppliers down to one. Instead of automatically renewing licenses, Accenture now subjects every commitment to critique, saving an average of US$50-60 million annually.

This list of ideas hardly exhausts the possibilities for value creation. Once you embrace the "less can be more" mindset, you will find yourself scrutinizing every corner of your IT function for overlooked inefficiencies and taken-for-granted redundancies.

Help others be more productive

IT is not the only departmental function that adds value to an enterprise. How effective would many organizations be without capable human resources, finance, or legal functions? IT frequently can leverage the power of technology to enable these other corporate departments to execute their work more effectively. Adding value by helping other functions become more productive is yet another way in which the IT operation can create value for the enterprise.

Here are just a few instances in which Accenture's CIO Organization has helped colleagues in other areas of Accenture do their jobs better, faster and cheaper:

Recruiting: Accenture's most valuable assets are clearly its people. Long before Accenture's global workforce passed the 200,000 mark, we recognized that we required a more technologically advanced approach than the company's home-grown systems. At one time, 45 highly localized staff-recruiting systems, often relying on manual data entry, had to process roughly one million résumés a year for review. In 2006, the CIO Organization collaborated with Accenture's human resources function to design and build an innovative new talent-acquisition system to keep pace with our aggressive growth. The new Accenture talent acquisition system – an automated, Web-based solution that runs in a software-as-a-service (SaaS) model with one, global data repository – made the recruiting process more consistent worldwide, and brought significant cost savings. It dramatically increased the efficiency and effectiveness of Accenture's recruiters and reduced the time between application and job offer, allowing us to attract talent faster, better serve our clients, and stay ahead of the competition.

Solution delivery: Accenture delivers a bewildering array of business solutions and services to clients all over the world. Despite this diversity, many Accenture engagements begin the same way: once we agree on the scope of a project with our client, we must mobilize and organize a vast global team to deliver the solutions or services required quickly, efficiently and effectively. In the past, organizing these complex engagements depended almost entirely on experienced Accenture executives, who did not always have the tools to match the task – sometimes nothing more sophisticated than a spreadsheet. Our CIO Organization saw an opportunity to help our client delivery teams through technology, and we got to work. A new tool we created – "Manage myEngagements" – was deployed in 2010 to help Accenture executives launch engagements more rapidly, and manage them with consistency and predictability. For the first time, capabilities for work and time, contracts, financials and resource management have been integrated in a single-instance global application. Instead of spreadsheets, the solution gives our executives common tools to break down complex work, source and manage resources, view metrics, monitor finances, and track costs. Previously, executives had to enter data manually; the new solution pulls accurate data directly from Accenture's master repository. Engagements once had work plans, forecasts and charge codes that were not linked; the new application helps our team leaders set up the work in the way they want to manage it, and then uses the same structures for budgeting and financial reporting. Clients are seeing new levels of accountability as Accenture teams more accurately track commitments. The new solution also lets Accenture report financial data the way clients need it. Accenture professionals gain from reduced administrative chores, freeing up more people to deliver greater value. Accenture's corporate performance is aided by more accurate financial reporting, better business intelligence, and enhanced risk management.

Help the entire enterprise

Going beyond point solutions, the IT function is uniquely positioned to help the entire organization become more productive. Take the explosion of collaboration technologies as a case in point. Today's social networking communities and Web 2.0 tools have captured the attention of enterprises everywhere. Advances in technologies and breakthroughs in collaboration promise easy connections, informal interaction, and help when you need it – classic small-office benefits on a global scale. Yet where do you start, how do you proceed, and when or where is the real pay-off?

Accenture has already made significant investments in these new technologies over the last several years, and is in the advanced stages of a pioneering implementation of communication and collaboration technologies for Accenture's entire global workforce. Launched in 2007, the program is ambitious in scale and approach, and focused on changing the way people work across Accenture and with clients around the world. Dubbed the "collaboration program", this effort is Accenture's response to a variety of trends at work in every global organization, beginning with a new generation of tech-savvy, mobile workers. Intent on finding solutions fast, today's workers expect access to the same networking tools at the office that they have at home. Our program is designed to make Accenture people more productive by providing comparable business capabilities and other innovative ways to connect and communicate with colleagues.

Here are just a few of the program's major features:

- Accenture now operates one of the world's largest private networks for high-definition videoconferencing. With more than 70 installations, and still expanding, Accenture's global network also provides direct access to clients and other companies using this technology.
- Virtually everyone in Accenture now has access to personal communication and collaboration tools, enabling our professionals to turn computers into phones, instantly see who is available and how best to reach them, and launch free and secure audio or video conference calls or desktop sharing with one-click, drag-and-drop ease.
- Business networking tools are rapidly spreading across Accenture, as users embrace affinity-style groups, microblogging and blogging as new online channels to enable swift and seamless global collaboration.

The immediate returns on these investments have been clear and convincing. More than 37 million minutes each month of peer-to-peer and conference audio calls within Accenture are now conducted fee-free via a voice over Internet protocol (VOIP) enabled personal communication interface. Over 5,000 hours of videoconferencing usage each month is also helping Accenture save millions of dollars in travel costs. Less quantifiable, but no less real, are the intangible benefits: gains in work-life balance experienced by Accenture professionals who travel less, and so can spend more time with their families without sacrificing on-the-job performance; increased efficiency, as people effectively pick the brains of their brightest colleagues through business networking tools; the overall advance in effectiveness resulting from greater collaboration across silos and geographies; and the growth of a more cohesive global organization with shared global values.

Reduce risk

For many corporations, the global financial crisis dramatized the importance of banks for operational survival. Corporate executives suddenly woke to the fact that banking relationships could turn into liabilities if their principal banks were unable to sustain normal activities. Payrolls could not be processed, hedging activities would be crimped, and the myriad other daily transactions required to keep companies funded and functioning might grind to a halt.

Exposure to this systemic risk was compounded by the proprietary technology systems linking bank and customer. These proprietary platforms made it difficult, if not impossible, for corporations to switch banks quickly or smoothly in a crunch. Companies now recognize the value of being able to change banks quickly, and of being less dependent on banking partners for daily cash needs.

Our IT team has helped Accenture manage these risks by collaborating with our treasury colleagues on the Accenture treasury transformation initiative, which does four things:

- Replace bank "plumbing" – the proprietary platforms that enable transactions – with more flexible solutions, so that Accenture can work with more banks more easily, and change banks quickly by moving to the

Society for Worldwide Interbank Financial Telecommunication (SWIFT).

- Move more transactions off proprietary banking platforms and onto the company's own financial systems, so that if a company uses SAP as its primary financial platform, vital treasury processes will also leverage the same solution.
- Move analytical tools, trading platforms and foreign exchange hedging capabilities inside the treasury function, so that corporate treasurers can execute these valuable strategies without the support of banks.
- Move to a streamlined settlement process among the various entities found in a typical global enterprise.

This initiative has already demonstrated its value inside Accenture. Would other companies be interested in the solution we have crafted? What would we need to do in order to commercialize the application we have developed? These are the types of questions we are exploring inside Accenture, and are the same questions IT functions in every enterprise should ask whenever they create something with marketable value.

Enable growth

Is your enterprise active in the financial services area? Few industries are more heavily dependent on IT. If manufacturing is your field, what large-scale enterprise is not directly reliant on IT-enabled shop floor automation? Whatever business sector your company is in, the chances are that IT can play an integral part in enabling or accelerating top-line enterprise growth and bottom-line profitability.

As Accenture grew from 75,000 to more than 215,000 employees over the past decade, the IT function was continually challenged to implement the new technology required to support it. A dramatically larger company – with more people, more diversification, and revenues that nearly doubled – placed enormous demands on our infrastructure. More and different types of businesses required new and different technology, and the scaling of existing technology to accommodate larger transaction volumes. The network transformation initiative discussed earlier, when Accenture completely redid its global communications network, was one example of the growth-enabling tools that IT brings to the table.

Inside Accenture, our internal IT function is continually collaborating with other parts of the business in evaluating new growth opportunities in areas such as business analytics and software development. Every year, Accenture's CIO Organization designs, builds and runs entirely new applications or adapts out-of-the-box applications to serve our internal business needs. In some instances, the solution we create for internal customers may also meet an important marketplace need.

Make smart value judgments

There is no shortage of areas in which value creation opportunities are readily found. Look no further than cloud computing, or device convergence among PCs, smart phones and netbooks. But before making a value-based investment decision on any given opportunity, you have to first make a smart value judgment.

For example, at Accenture we believe that it is strategically smarter to add value by focusing on entirely new capabilities than by tweaking existing ones. You can spend – and waste – a lot of money making minor revisions and enhancements to existing capabilities. The newly released and "enhanced" tool or application may run a little bit better, but is it so improved as to justify the investment, and is the incremental improvement starving other investments of quantum-leap capabilities? At the risk of generalizing, extensive releases of the same basic tool may add useful improvements, but are not likely to deliver a step-function change. You eventually reach a point at which the only serious strategic option is to step back, tear down what exists, and start from scratch. Making a smart value judgment about when you have arrived at that point is the essence of IT management.

When we look at technology investments inside Accenture's CIO Organization, we strive to examine upfront whether or not our investment can be justified by a return in hard-dollar benefits, or whether the rationale for our investment will be framed in more strategic terms. Tempting though it may be to insist always on the monetary return, there are certain types of investments that cannot be justified by short-term return on investment (ROI) calculations, but will yield valuable strategic gains over the long haul.

Our experience with the re-platforming of Accenture's internal portal illustrates the difference between incremental improvements and categorical gains. Several years ago, Accenture, like many enterprises, introduced the Accenture portal as a central source of information for our global workforce. Since its launch, continuing advances in web technology now make it feasible to support a totally customizable portal environment – one in which the user gets to decide what information they need, and then choose the information organization and display that best meets their individual working style.

In evaluating the next stage of the Accenture portal, we could have stayed with what we had, making only minor improvements. But Accenture's human resources department, in collaboration with the CIO Organization, concluded that the new, fully personal portal would make our people more productive by making it easier for them to find information and manage their tasks and schedules. Even though it was difficult to put a hard-dollar value on the savings of five or ten minutes worth of employee time a day, we felt that the step-change migration to a totally personalized platform made sense, and so we went ahead.

Communicate the value you create

It is always a good thing to create value for your enterprise. So why not share the good news with all of IT's key stakeholders? It amazes me to realize how many IT professionals I encounter who do a magnificent job with value creation, but when it comes to value communication fail to make their case as completely and persuasively as they could. After you have exploited every opportunity to do things better, faster and cheaper, and then gone on to exploit many of the other value opportunities we have discussed, you should seal the deal for your IT function by letting the world know about your success.

Perhaps the explanation for such an obvious yet mysterious lapse is the simple fact that people do not automatically think they need to communicate when it comes to IT. Our experience inside Accenture suggests exactly the opposite. High-performance IT is all about changing the way people work, for the better. Wherever people and change are involved, the communications discipline must be central to the process. Therefore, each of our IT initiatives within Accenture is not complete without carefully planned communications and change management support.

We begin with the basics: who are our key audiences, what are our key messages, and how will we effectively convey those messages to our targets? Whether the message concerns a service outage or the deployment of new capabilities, we make the standard tools and techniques of communications and change management an integral part of every implementation. When we introduce new tools and applications, rather than simply putting a new tool out there and waiting for word-of-mouth to spread the news, we actively promote user adoption with all the means at our disposal: dedicated microsites filled with support information, podcasts and webcasts, custom-created communications targeting specific user groups, promotional videos featuring satisfied user testimonials, and every other technique in the marketing communications toolkit.

The collaboration program described earlier in this chapter exemplifies the vital role that communications plays whenever you are talking about using IT to change the way people work together. With more than 15 distinct tools in the collaboration initiative, we invested as much time and effort driving user adoption of the tools as we did launching them in the first place. A critical component in our approach to change management was the recognition that changing the ways people communicate and connect with one another on a daily basis is as complex an assignment as any change management challenge.

Not surprisingly, the "selling" of the collaboration program involved a great deal of collaboration in itself. Colleagues in change management, internal communications, marketing communications and IT worked together to create a dedicated internal Accenture microsite that was the central promotional focus for information. With this microsite as a clearinghouse for news, the team sponsored community meetings, placed hundreds of articles in internal Accenture publications and websites, and sustained a high profile for the effort through monthly company-wide e-mails, adoption "competitions" among organization units, viral videos and promotional videos.

Here are some of the lessons learned in communications and change management that may be of use for other enterprises considering a similar journey:

- Sponsorship support should be secured at the highest possible levels within affected business units, so the change is not an IT initiative, but rather a business initiative.
- IT, change management, internal communications and marketing professionals should be brought together to create a unified change effort.
- An integrated and consistently branded communications strategy should be employed for the overall program, rather than launching many individual vehicles.
- Distinctive launch communications and comprehensive training needs to be created.
- Specific use cases for collaboration tools should be developed to encourage adoption, and early adopters should be identified as your change agents.
- Collaboration tools need to be integrated into existing business processes and functions.

- The adoption of tools and technologies should be tracked, and additional support delivered wherever variances suggest obstacles to adoption.

Moving beyond deployment and adoption to strategic communications, we continually seek to inform executive leadership and other key audiences about new capabilities, client success stories, user testimonials, and the tangible value being created for the enterprise through effective investment in IT. We, of course, report on a scheduled basis to Accenture's senior leadership, using such tools as our IT strategic performance scorecard *(see Figure 14 in Chapter 3)*.

The important point to note is that reporting and accountability do not simply travel upward to our superiors. Since we also view our internal customers as the "boss," we believe we have a responsibility to let them know how we are performing. Communications specialists – who are an integral part of the IT organization – design message architectures that segment our audiences, and tailor the messages to be conveyed to each distinct group. The emphasis, throughout, is always on the substantive measures of performance achieved and value delivered, rather than mere promotion. The communications effort extends to the development of an annual report on IT programs, this created for both our internal customers and for Accenture's external customers who are interested in how we are going about the business of IT.

Running IT like a business

Talk therapy

What is the best way to create a value mindset inside the IT function, especially if you and most of your IT colleagues have spent your careers with a cost-center mentality? I would recommend talk therapy. Get outside the IT department on a regular scheduled basis, talk to your customers, and ask them what their needs are. It is astonishing to discover how many IT teams do not do this, or fail to do it in a comprehensive way. The simple act of talking to people at senior levels, and every other level, can change your worldview, broadening your perspective on IT to include what it does – or should – bring to the table. When we are engaged in our regular IT strategy update at Accenture, we sit down to interview 50-60 counterparts across the company, at middle management as well as senior levels. We learn a tremendous amount from our internal customers about what value really means. In the process, we build stronger business relationships. In one such conversation, we were told that we were one of the first groups that ever bothered to ask what they needed . . . usually, these customers were just told what they were going to get or needed to do. These conversations are also invaluable for informing people about our process of identifying investment opportunities. The more you meet and talk, the more you will learn about the value you can bring to your enterprise.

CHAPTER 5: TRICKS OF THE TRADE FOR RUNNING IT LIKE A BUSINESS

You need sound principles to run any business, even the IT function, and we have attempted to set forth the basic principles that have withstood the test of time inside Accenture's IT operation. But principles alone are not enough to help you meet the demands of everyday business realities. Principles must be tempered by pragmatic business experience and practical business sense. In this chapter, we discuss a number of tricks of the trade that have worked well for Accenture's IT function. These techniques and practices may prove to be valuable for your enterprise as well.

Flexible resources

Silos are the stealthy enemies of any organization: they tend to add duplicative processes and people, as though each and every silo had to be equipped as a freestanding business unit. To combat this tendency, we recognized within Accenture's IT function that certain skills were broadly applicable across the entire IT organization, and could be deployed from place to place across projects and programs as circumstances warranted. Rather than create and staff permanent positions for each new initiative we undertook, we created deployable resource groups, which essentially are like mini consulting teams within Accenture's internal IT operation.

For larger enterprises with scale and deep resources, these deployable teams add flexibility as well as capability to the

IT manager's toolkit. Take change management as an example. Not every IT program or initiative requires deep change management expertise, so to staff and support multiple standing change management teams would be wasteful. But change-intensive projects that affect large numbers of users most certainly demand high levels of change management expertise in order to be effective. Thus, it is far better to create a deep-skilled change management capability, and then allocate this resource to those projects that require a high level of proficiency.

At Accenture, we recently introduced a new solution to one of the company's key corporate functions. The new tool was vital to operations, but the actual change only affected about 150 people. Managing the change was a task that the project team was well able to handle alongside its implementation chores. Contrast this with Accenture's collaboration initiative, which has been implemented over several years, has introduced over 15 specific tools, and affects the way every single Accenture professional works around the world. Change management was essential to promote adoption of the new collaboration technologies, which is why our deployable change management team was a key part of the collaboration initiative from the beginning.

Program and project management is another area where deployable resource teams have paid valuable dividends in efficiency and effectiveness. The deployable resource group in this discipline is less focused on a particular technology or functional area, allowing its members to concentrate almost exclusively on the task of planning, managing and keeping projects on track.

So, the next time you face a management situation where you do not have enough specific work in a given area to keep a dedicated team busy on a full-time basis, consider creating and using a flexible resources group that is shared across the entire IT organization.

IT human resources model – positions and roles

Most jobs in IT organizations are position-based, with each position being defined by a job description, responsibilities, and specific skill requirements. In this system, when an opening needs to be filled, the applicant with the best specific skills tends to get the position. Several years ago, Accenture's IT function was staffed in precisely this manner. Then we noticed a disquieting trend. When a spot opened up, someone else on the same team usually had the most similar specific skills, and so that individual got the job. Meanwhile, outstanding people who were available, but currently working in other areas, were not considered for promotion. We discovered that we were not promoting our best people, just the best available individuals with specific skill sets. We felt that we had to keep the position-based organizational structure, but at the same time give people a way to acquire more experience and pursue their careers in Accenture IT with greater flexibility.

The solution devised was to redefine "position-based" in certain broad areas, and to introduce a new concept of "role." In the new model, positions are tied to personnel levels and broad competence areas, such as application development. Roles define operational responsibilities on particular projects, and are to be filled by qualified individuals.

For instance, an individual holding the position of "business application development specialist" could work in many "roles," such as on a financial services project, on a project refreshing the *www.accenture.com* website, or on the Accenture portal. The individual holds one position – as a business application development specialist – but could fill many roles by moving from project to project and area to area, gaining experience and expertise along the way.

This concept of developing broad competence areas and more high-level positions with many specific roles has enabled us to change the focus in filling positions from finding the one individual with very specific skills to finding the person with the best skills in the broader competence area. We are now able to post available positions more broadly, and invite applications from anyone with the broader competence.

For instance, if we need to fill five new positions in the area of business applications development, we are able to accept applications from anyone with business application development competence. The change entails tolerating a slightly longer learning curve for the applicant in the new role, since there is no longer so exclusive a focus on particular skills in the specific area. But that price is worth paying in return for the chance to give people more opportunities to try different areas of IT.

This change has benefited the organization as well as individual IT professionals. New people have brought fresh perspectives to different areas of the IT function. The change also works as well with senior executives as with specialists and analysts.

Employee engagement

Moving beyond the professional development of individual employees, Accenture's IT organization has made a concerted effort to raise employee engagement by creating opportunities for people to provide input to leadership, develop as leaders, and improve the organization. The Accenture IT employee councils – groups of 10 to 12 representatives drawn from both non-management and management levels of the global IT team – have been valuable vehicles for improving the working environment for our people. Employee councils located in Chicago and Spain collaborate with one another to discuss opportunities to improve the IT organization and make it a best-in-class workplace for our IT people, addressing topics such as cultural differences, employee recognition, and career opportunities. The councils, in turn, organize task forces to deal with specific projects. These councils review the results of our annual employee engagement survey, and make recommendations on behalf of the IT workforce. Suggestions from the councils have led to the creation of employee recognition programs that recognize outstanding individuals and high-performance IT teams.

Other examples of activities promoting employee engagement that are familiar features of many enterprises include career fairs designed to promote awareness of career options, and cultural awareness days intended to bridge the natural distances in a global workforce by encouraging a broader understanding of diverse cultures and backgrounds.

Managing suppliers and contracts

Many companies sell excellent tools for testing software. Left to their own devices, your different project teams will invariably select different testing tools, based on prior experiences and personal preference. In my view, you will be far better off negotiating one contract with a single vendor for a set price than you will be by working with multiple vendors – assuming all the solutions offer comparable capabilities.

Take this same equation and multiply it across an entire IT function, and it is easy to see why the management of suppliers and contracts is one of the simplest ways of saving significant sums. I know from experience, because in the first year I was responsible for supplier and contract management, we used supplier and contract rationalization to save Accenture millions of dollars.

All of this is basic business common sense: standardize usage with a single provider, consolidate multiple contracts with the same vendor, and use your purchasing power to negotiate the best possible price and terms and conditions that support your business. As common-sense as this is, it is nevertheless astonishing how many IT functions fail to take advantage of these basics of good business practice.

Consider your current practices with automatic renewals of maintenance contracts. Do you know if the value you are getting from the contract is commensurate with the cost? If the application is solid and stable, is the current level of maintenance support necessary? How mission-critical is a particular application, and what is the business impact if the application happens to be down for a limited period of time? In the absence of critical oversight on the cost of maintenance, everyone's tendency is to err on the side of the highest possible level of support, which invariably happens to be the most expensive option. So critiquing maintenance renewals is one area where low-hanging fruit abounds.

Smart management of suppliers and contracts presupposes that you actually know the suppliers and contracts you currently have. Not every IT function has this level of visibility into its suppliers and contracts, which can number in the hundreds or thousands. When you ask for a list of current contracts or committed spend, and the response is that this information is not readily available, you know that you have to get back to basics and begin building rigor and discipline into this critical business process.

Planning and resource management

In the past, when you scanned the marketplace for useful solutions for running IT like a business, you would have seen either project management tools or large-scale enterprise resource planning (ERP) platforms for finance or human resources management, with very few choices in between. Tools that link project reporting to organizational reporting and then on to enterprise-level reporting have been limited, which does much to explain why most companies do not have the architecture in place to support planning and resource management of an IT function.

At Accenture, we bridged this gap by building our own custom-developed tool – the Solution Management System (SMS) – as a business commitment and financial and resource management solution. For our people running the internal IT business day to day, it provides a way to tie our business commitments to our financial plans and resource plans, which is fully integrated with our project management tools and our ERP platform. SMS automatically pulls project-level information up to financial and human resources systems, and also pulls down information from the ERP platform, giving the people who are actually running the business the information and analytics capability they need.

We do not want to take financial and human resources responsibilities away from our project managers, because they would then tend to focus on only the technical aspects of the jobs. We want people to run their particular part of the IT function like they are running an actual business, employing the same financial prudence, exercising judgment about allocating resources, and dealing with expectations of how much projects will cost and what resources will be required.

Adding this "middleware" to tie traditional project management tools to enterprise level ERP platforms, and providing the ability to link the IT organization's business commitments to our financial and resource plans, allows our management to truly run our IT function like a business.

To capitalize or to expense?

Many IT organizations tend to let the finance department determine how they capitalize internal software and technology development projects. Facing generally accepted accounting principles (GAAP) on what you can capitalize and what you can expense, and being left to their own devices, financial managers will generally tend to capitalize everything that can be capitalized, creating an asset that is put on the corporate books. The reason why is simple: current expenditures are treated as capital investments, rather than operating expenses.

The danger with this approach is that once an asset has been booked, you will, in future years, have to depreciate that asset and pay depreciation and internal interest charges against it. By capitalizing all your major software and technology development programs, you eventually paint your IT function into a fiscal corner.

At Accenture, we went down this path in the early years of our transformational journey, when we were building a large number of assets. In the short term, capitalization helped us financially by reducing our operating expenses. After a year or two, we began to see increasing percentages of our budget tied up in non-discretionary depreciation and interest charges. The more assets we created, the more we had to pay in depreciation and interest charges, and the greater the percentage of our budget became fixed and non-discretionary.

Making matters worse, once you have put the asset on your books, you have to make sure that the asset still has the same value as the value on the corporate ledger. You soon find yourself attending seemingly endless asset impairment review meetings, at which people debate the value of some small development project completed years ago.

At Accenture, our solution to this issue has been to expense almost everything. We worked with our finance department and our auditors and set a high threshold for capitalization of internal IT projects; if a technology development initiative does not meet the threshold, we will expense it. Since we have done this, the number of assets we are depreciating is down to some seven to eight annually. In effect, we have taken the large, fixed cost of depreciation and interest – that was approaching 40% of our budget – and turned it into a variable expense. We now have the ability to ramp up or ramp down our spending as needed, as opposed to the situation of being locked into fixed costs before the fiscal year even begins.

Becoming addicted to capitalization is easy; getting off this accounting drug is painful. You essentially get hit twice: by depreciation and interest on projects that were capitalized, as well as current projects being expensed, until those assets become fully depreciated and drop off your books. If we had it to do over again, we would have set a high threshold for project capitalization from the beginning.

Audit and regulatory compliance management

Audit and regulatory compliance is a growing global phenomenon and, when not managed properly, a potentially burdensome business responsibility for IT organizations.

In the IT portion of a company's annual financial audit, external auditors examine the appropriateness of controls around technologies such as an ERP platform that could have an impact on financial reporting. Auditors are also interested in examining internal controls around production code, procedures for migrating from test environments to production environments, and controls for production environments as well. Companies that do business with governments as clients are subject to additional regulations and audits to confirm appropriate rates for costs and overhead, evidence of contract compliance, security controls around the IT environment, and more.

Unaided, audit teams will go directly to whatever IT group in the enterprise is directly responsible for the IT processes involved in the audit. This can result in a cacophony of audit requests, as IT teams are hit with similar or duplicative requests from both internal and external sources.

To avoid such confusion, Accenture created a centralized team for all audit and compliance-related activities. This central team is responsible for coordinating all audit activities for the entire IT organization.

The operational benefits of this centralized approach are as obvious to our IT teams as they are to external auditors. The IT team understands the importance of the audit, can plan for it in advance, and is prepared with the necessary information when the audit commences. Auditors are equally pleased with the approach, which minimizes the need to explain audit procedures repeatedly with multiple teams. This approach allows our IT teams to focus on the work at hand and get business value from the increased rigor of our IT controls, while off-loading the coordination and planning work associated with audit and regulatory activities to a central team who are experts in the area.

Running IT like a business

Change as fast as you can

When it comes to change, how much is too much, and how fast is too fast? In the field of information technology, where change is not just constant but continuously accelerating, the pace of change has practical implications. How quickly can systems be switched without compromising dependability? How

---

easily can your workforce understand, accept and adapt to new technologies being introduced, especially if that workforce is distributed across countries and cultures? At what point does change stop being constructive and start creating chaotic conditions?

As Accenture worked its way through a decade of transformational change in its IT function, it wrestled with these issues. In many instances, we were excited at the compelling business case offered by a new technology, but were hesitant to ask our own internal team to take on yet another major implementation, not to mention the end users, who had to accept a new way of doing things or change the tools they were using.

From a purely financial perspective, we look back over the 10-year timeline and see that, if we had it to do all over again – and knew at the outset how significant the returns would be on our IT investment – we would have done everything that we did *even faster*. We discovered that our internal IT team was ready for any challenge we put before them. We also discovered how receptive and responsive Accenture professionals were to new technologies. Even when we felt our people might need a pause, they told us that they loved the new tools we were introducing, and clamored for more.

Each enterprise is different, to be sure, and regulating the pace of change is a critical management responsibility demanding keen judgment on the part of business executives. But whenever I am asked if an IT organization should change as fast as it can, my answer is, "Yes!"

CHAPTER 6: TOWARD HIGH-PERFORMANCE IT

Over the course of this book, I have attempted to map the steps required to run IT like a business. But running IT in a business-like fashion is not an end in itself; the goal is something greater still – high-performance IT.

Accenture's proprietary research into high-performance IT has drawn a clear cause-and-effect relationship between high-performance IT and high performance across the entire enterprise. As you map your IT function's transformational journey, keep this ultimate destination in view. Whether you decide to incrementally change over an extended time period, or make a single concerted push in transforming your IT function, high-performance IT is the destination that counts.

CIOs understand that, as expectations across the entire executive leadership rise in the new economy, they have a newfound opportunity to position IT as a partner – and a growth engine – for the business. The desire is there: Accenture research shows that 67% of CIOs want to position IT as a strategic asset, thereby creating differentiated business capabilities for their organizations.

Whether they can stretch to this strategic level, however, remains to be seen. For years, executive leadership teams have been setting a higher bar for IT, challenging CIOs to deliver IT capabilities that fuel business innovation and agility. But in many instances, CIOs have not met the challenge. Some IT leaders continue to feel hamstrung by a combination of cost-cutting mandates, inadequate skill development in their IT organizations, and a "keep the lights on" focus that permeates many IT organizations.

There are, however, a few exceptions. High-performing IT organizations have demonstrated excellence in three key traits – innovation, agility and execution – which enable them not only to manage IT like a business, but to run IT for the business and with the business. CIOs at these organizations are engaged in their company's business strategies and are able to truly map out how IT supports those strategies.

The latest results from Accenture's ongoing high-performance IT research show that high performers don't just do a few things well – they excel across the board.

For example, compared with their peers, high performers:

- Have web-enabled 42% more of their customer interactions and 93% more of their supplier interactions
- Are 44% more likely to recognize the strategic role IT plays in customer satisfaction
- Are eight times more likely to consistently measure the benefits realized from strategic IT initiatives
- Spend 29% more annually on developing and implementing new applications, rather than on maintaining existing ones
- Are twice as likely to view workforce performance as a priority.

Notably, the gap between high performers and other IT organizations is widening. When it comes to innovation, the delta between high performers and their peers has grown from 31% in 2008 to 42%. When the issue is execution, the gap has risen seven points – from 30% to 37% – in just two years. High performers that showed an ability to differentiate their core IT capabilities during the downturn – a period when most organizations were focused primarily on cost-cutting – are now positioned to deliver much more value to their companies as they search for business growth.

The widening performance gap between high performers and other IT organizations should serve as a wake-up call for the underperformers to improve core capabilities – or risk being marginalized by business leadership. The message is clear: the power to change is in the CIO's hands. CIOs can accept a role as a caretaker for the business, or they can begin taking steps to improve the agility, innovativeness and execution of their IT organizations in order to establish a stronger partnership with the business. These steps can help them bridge not only the gap that exists between their organizations and high performers, but also the fissure that, in many companies, continues to separate IT.

What are high performers doing differently? Since its inception, Accenture's ongoing high-performance IT research program has shown that some IT organizations perform fundamentally differently and continuously better than their peers.

This high performance is exhibited across three IT building blocks:

IT execution: Leaders in IT execution have active governance programs and involve the business as a partner in the IT strategy. They use metrics to ensure the effective cost/benefits management of IT investments and manage IT like a business.

IT agility: Leaders in IT agility are effective at aligning IT resources to business requirements and priorities. They integrate their optimized applications portfolio internally and externally, and they seek technologies that provide dynamic access to infrastructure.

IT innovation: Leaders in IT innovation consider IT a strategic asset for competitive advantage in the application of a continuous innovation and collaboration mindset to the deployment of new technologies.

These building blocks cut across nine core capabilities, which range from application architecture to workforce management. To be sure, each of these capabilities poses unique and ongoing challenges to all IT organizations. High performers, however, have leveraged these capabilities more effectively to refocus their efforts on meeting core business objectives – such as customer satisfaction and employee productivity – while other IT organizations continue to view cost management as a top priority. In many ways, it's tough to blame them. The constraints of legacy infrastructures and a mandate to reduce operational costs can cloud a CIO's strategic thinking, as well as how to spend their time and budget. The high performers in our survey, however, have embraced these challenges and created pockets of excellence that show demonstrable results across nine core capabilities, which our research explores in detail.

1. Strategic IT alignment

While all CIOs recognize that IT is strategic to the business agenda now more than ever before, only a fraction of CIOs – the high performers in our 2010 research – are better at defining how IT can help achieve core business objectives and then deliver on those objectives. For example, they are more than three times as likely to deliver IT's committed value in new products and services, and twice as likely to cite IT's strategic role in improving employee productivity.

To help the business achieve its goals, high performers are investing heavily in application development: 70% of their resources are devoted to deploying, testing, integrating, building or enhancing applications. This means they are spending more time building new functionality and less time "keeping the lights on."

Investing in new technologies is critical for businesses looking to improve their agility in the new economy. High performers, in fact, are on average 25% more likely than other IT organizations to deploy or pilot new technologies, and even more in areas such as business analytics, virtualization, and data management and security.

More specifically related to the use of emerging web tools that reduce costs, streamline, or otherwise improve interactions with employees, customers and suppliers, high performers have 93% more web-enabled supplier interactions and 42% more web-enabled customer interactions, compared with other IT organizations. In addition, twice as many employee interactions are mobile-enabled.

2. Governance

The economic downturn forced many IT organizations to cut spending in proportion to the reduced revenues of the business. But high performers have shown resilience in securing new investments, in large part because of their excellence in IT governance and their ability to turn cost savings and efficiency improvements into value-adding reinvestments in IT.

For example, 69% of high performers say they develop a business case for nearly every new IT initiative – more than twice the percentage of other IT organizations. Perhaps more importantly, high performers are eight times more likely to measure the benefits realized from these IT projects.

Among all respondents, on average 55% of IT projects are delivered successfully annually. This shows an improvement over industry reported benchmarks, and much of the credit can be given to the knowledge, practices, and standards that have contributed to the professionalization of the IT organization. Unfortunately, too many failures still occur. Because many of these failures can be traced to management and decision-making practices, it is useful to explore the tools and best practices IT organizations use to help diagnose and perhaps even prevent failures from occurring.

3. Application architecture

A critical distinction between companies identified as 2010 high performers and others can be made in terms of how the target application architecture of IT organizations are defined and evolve. The IT leaders emphasize the importance of a target application architecture centered on three objectives.

The first involves scheduling and implementing regular refreshes of the application architecture: 62% of high performers cited this element as highly important, compared with 17% of other IT organizations.

The second involves proactively applying architecture principles in all initiatives. More than 60% of high performers said this objective was highly important, compared with 33% of the other respondents.

Thirdly, high performers understand the importance of avoiding duplication in their application portfolios: 54% cited this feature as highly important, versus 35% of other IT organizations.

High performers are in control of the evolution of their architecture toward emerging concepts, such as virtualization and service orientation. They also effectively manage the tradeoffs between the desire to innovate and the incremental costs associated with exploration and innovation. One third of high performers tell us they retire less successful services quickly to manage costs, while only six percent of other organizations are able to do so.

As Accenture's research clearly shows, architecture is the IT organization's weakest link for most participants. Organizations should focus on building stronger and more active application and technology architecture capabilities, with IT and business stakeholders working together to adopt and enforce consistent processes to plan, execute and optimize investments across the organization that directly support business value creation. This architecture should be refreshed and optimized regularly.

4. Information management

High performers, unsurprisingly, are more evolved in their information management practices than other IT organizations. They are more than twice as likely, for example, to have developed target data architectures, and created effective business intelligence and analytics capabilities, as well as data governance. High performers also provide their employees with more access to the most detailed and real-time information they need to do their jobs. The most accessible, granular and real-time customer data, for example, is 80% more accessible, more than twice as granular, and twice as likely to be available in real time in high-performing IT organizations compared with other IT organizations.

Investments in information management technology are delivering significantly more value for high performers. More than three quarters of high performers said that business analytics investments are delivering 75% or more of the expected value, versus only 40% in other IT organizations. For example, high performers have invested more aggressively in data quality assurance and master data management technologies, giving them reliable and consistent information about customers, products, employees, and suppliers. Indeed, 92% and 77% of high performers have deployed or are piloting data quality assurance and master data management, respectively, versus 53% and 57% of other organizations.

5. Service management and operations

IT organizations are changing the way they provide and manage IT services – high performers most notably, as they progress toward achieving centralized and fully virtualized environments. Having rationalized and simplified their IT for a leaner infrastructure, high performers provide IT services via a standard, well-defined services-based catalog at twice the rate of other IT organizations, for example. In addition, almost half of high performers are leveraging advanced virtualization technologies and dynamic provisioning, versus just three percent of other IT organizations in our research.

Adopting standards-based services catalogs and deploying virtualization technologies puts high performers in a much better position to migrate enterprise infrastructure and applications to private or public cloud services, as the need arises. While external cloud services represent just a modest fraction of their infrastructure, three times as many high performers as other organizations are looking to leverage these dynamic services as needed today.

High performers are also ahead of their peers in their approach to monitoring IT operations. For example, 70% say they measure end-to-end business process performance with automated, live reporting, versus 23% of other IT organizations.

6. Solutions delivery

High performers are significantly ahead in extracting benefits from the integration of business processes, information and IT systems. For example, they are six times more likely to provide real-time visibility into processes, and four times more likely to provide real-time dashboards and alert systems. In addition, as noted earlier, high performers spend 29% more annually on developing and implementing applications than they spend on running them – a significant enabler of innovation and business agility. This approach also allows leading IT organizations to ensure applications meet their technical and business needs: on average, high performers' applications are more than two times as likely to meet their business needs and more than three times as likely to meet their technical needs.

7. Workforce and resource management

IT organizations are investing in developing leadership, while focusing on setting a clear IT direction and priorities. Moreover, they strive to assign the right people to the right roles, and reward them according to set objectives tied to business outcomes.

For example:

- More than a quarter of IT organizations seek to deploy their IT resources in a supply/demand model (also known as "on demand"), with most IT resources and services shared across business areas.
- Today, just under one in ten IT organizations measure their IT workforce performance against individual achievement and alignment with business outcomes, but 36% are hoping to achieve this objective in the future.
- One in six IT organizations actively seeks to create a well-managed IT workforce by aligning training and succession planning with workers' specific skills. Almost half of IT organizations plan on doing so in the future.

The high performers in our research make workforce management a top priority and have made significant strides in addressing workforce challenges. It is clear that high performers view the workforce strategically as a core resource – one that must be invested in and supported with the proper tools, training and certification. For example, high performers are more than seven times more likely than other IT organizations to have already invested in new technology skills development. They are six times as likely as other IT organizations to have a plan in place to address the aging workforce and the potential loss of institutional knowledge as these workers retire, three times more likely to be developing new career tracks to develop future IT workers, and three times more likely to be addressing skills development for application and technology architectures and information management.

8. *Information and technology security*

Security policies and procedures affect the entire business – its operations, how it interacts with customers and partners, and even its brand performance. High performers, which are more likely to have a chief security officer in place (with a clear role in the organization that is complementary to and reinforces the role of the CIO), demonstrate leadership and agility in deploying comprehensive information and technology security strategies. The majority of high performers (77%) also feel they have the right level of investment in security today, while 27% of other organizations believe they are under-investing in security initiatives. High performers are three times as likely to coordinate security governance with lines of business, as opposed to simply sharing security policies with them. High performers also put significantly more emphasis than other IT organizations on defining an overall security strategy and architecture: they are twice as likely, for instance, to implement data protection controls, and nearly three times as likely to automate compliance procedures and clarify a security governance model and organization structure.

9. *Outsourcing*

Outsourcing is more than just a way to lower costs. High-performing IT organizations strategically use outsourcing to gain access to critical IT skills, improve their agility and flexibility, increase the effectiveness of business processes, and lower the total cost of ownership of applications and infrastructure. High performers approach outsourcing as a partnership with service providers, which enables them to extract significantly more value out of their application and infrastructure investments. Out of the high performers in our research, 83% said application development and maintenance services provide the greatest value in helping them achieve critical IT objectives, while three quarters cited infrastructure management as providing high value in achieving IT goals.

Outsourcing also is a critical aspect to workforce management because it allows CIOs to build new skills faster and retire skills that are no longer relevant. High-performing IT organizations realize significantly more value from staff augmentation and, in fact, often meet or exceed their original objectives. This is in stark contrast to other IT organizations that do not leverage outsourcing.

Importantly, high performers are more successful at employing sophisticated metrics and processes to track the effectiveness of outsourcing service providers. For example, three quarters of high performers in our 2010 research said they employ sophisticated metrics for application outsourcing, compared with 36% of other IT organizations in our survey. High performers are also more likely to employ sophisticated metrics for infrastructure outsourcing (73%, compared with 46% of other organizations) and business process outsourcing (67% versus 35%). These metrics are essential for demonstrating the value that outsourcing delivers to the business. While many organizations use inadequate process standardization and insufficient tools as excuses for not applying the necessary metrics, high performers are confident that their metrics demonstrate business value, particularly in infrastructure outsourcing and business process outsourcing. As a result, the value high performers realize from outsourced services more often exceeds their original projected business objectives.

What can we learn from these results? Business and IT leaders should continually be challenging the status quo by evaluating alternative computing models and emerging technologies – such as SaaS, cloud computing or mobility – as a means to reduce costs and improve employee efficiency, as well as to increase customer satisfaction. But we know that investing in new technologies alone will not make an organization a high performer.

It is worth restating that, by definition, high-performing IT organizations must excel across all three IT building blocks: execution, agility and innovation. In other words, high-performing IT organizations remain focused on the opportunity to improve IT value and gain competitive advantage, while improving IT's economics. High performers also understand that these are not mutually exclusive goals, meaning that improving in one area will help them improve performance in the other two as well. We believe that this virtuous cycle of performance improvement explains much of the widening gap between high performers and other organizations. CIOs have the power to close the performance gap and turn the vicious cycle into a virtuous one. Although there is no universal formula for becoming a high performer, there is a path that organizations can follow, regardless of their current state.

For more information about Accenture's high performance research, and for the full report on high-performance IT cited in this chapter, visit *www.accenture.com*. The Accenture Institute for High Performance develops and publishes practical insights into critical management issues and global economic trends. Its worldwide team of researchers connects with Accenture's consulting, technology and outsourcing leaders to demonstrate how organizations become and remain high performers through original, rigorous research and analysis.

Running IT like a business

You are never done

Even the most ambitiously drafted and carefully planned transformation program can never escape a fundamental reality about the business of IT. By the time we had implemented the latest platform at Accenture, we found that it was already time to start looking at the next generation of innovations. After we had completed the transformation of our network, and dramatically increased bandwidth, we rapidly saw traffic expand to fill the available capacity –faster than we imagined possible. The flip side of Moore's Law is that there will always be a tool, a trick or a technological solution better than the one you have. As fast as we believe our current computers are, scientists are already hard at work trying to build practical versions of quantum computers that, in theory, could deliver greater computing power than anything we can conceive of today. So when it comes to IT, even when you are finished, you are never done.

CHAPTER 7: ACCENTURE'S IT JOURNEY

In the preceding chapters, I have attempted to set forth the basic principles required to run IT like a business by drawing on lessons we learned at Accenture over the past decade, as we worked to transform our own IT operation. Along the way, we have talked about IT strategy and governance, managed services, and performance metrics, among other topics.

By now, a reader will quite rightly want to know how all this learning at Accenture translated into actual performance. You might be thinking, "What results did you actually achieve when you ran IT like a business?" In this chapter, I will endeavor to answer that question.

Our corporate heritage

When we at Accenture began building what we think of as a high-performance IT operation back in the year 2000, we did not clearly see our destination. So this has very much been a journey. In retrospect, the journey may appear to be neat and clean, but there were many twists and detours along the way. So it is useful to take the measure of where we were when we began, and where we stand today.

We began the journey with one major advantage and one potentially greater disadvantage. Both were related to our origins as a company, so allow me to begin the story with a little corporate history.

Our great advantage is that, at Accenture, technology in general and information technology in particular is part of our corporate DNA. The history of Accenture is, to a great extent, the history of global business consulting and information technology services over the past half century.

The creation of Accenture

The newly created company named "Accenture" came into being on a very rapid timetable. Inside the IT function, we had begun preparing for independent systems as early as 1999. Nevertheless, with legacy systems inherited from our former parent company, we faced the immediate need to define our IT strategy going forward and to build entirely independent technology capabilities. You might think it an exaggeration to claim that we had to start a new IT function from scratch, but apart from our making a copy of business applications, that was essentially the case. We had to put in place a new network, new data centers and hosting capabilities, help desks and all the other things required for a fully-functioning IT department.

In 2001, we had about 75,000 employees. We had absolutely no idea that Accenture would go on to have upwards of 215,000 employees, but we had ambitious growth strategies, and we knew we needed the IT infrastructure to support that growth. So we went to work.

The timeline shown in Figure 17 traces the journey we set off on, beginning with the immediate tasks related to the establishment of an independent base technology capability. Creating a solid foundation consumed a significant amount of energy and resources over the next few years, on top of which we, along with everyone else, also had to contend with the explosive growth of the Internet, the intensive countdown to the non-event that was the millennium bug, and the dot-com boom and bust.

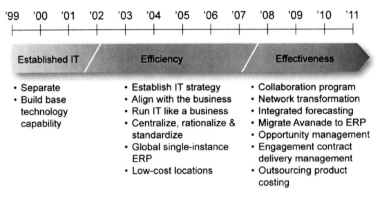

| '99 | '00 | '01 | '02 | '03 | '04 | '05 | '06 | '07 | '08 | '09 | '10 | '11 |

Established IT / **Efficiency** / **Effectiveness**

- Separate
- Build base technology capability

- Establish IT strategy
- Align with the business
- Run IT like a business
- Centralize, rationalize & standardize
- Global single-instance ERP
- Low-cost locations

- Collaboration program
- Network transformation
- Integrated forecasting
- Migrate Avanade to ERP
- Opportunity management
- Engagement contract delivery management
- Outsourcing product costing

Figure 17: Timeline for Accenture's transformational IT journey

From efficiency to effectiveness

After we had addressed the immediate priorities, the emphasis within the IT function shifted to running the IT function as efficiently as we possibly could. Many of the principles that drive running IT like a business were first formulated, tried and refined during this period. We were supporting some 600 global applications, over 1,500 local applications, multiple networks, a large number of data centers, and multiple technology platforms. We therefore set out with a vengeance to centralize, rationalize and standardize, because we saw how burdensome this complexity already was, and we knew the problems would only keep multiplying over time. Major progress was made when we moved Accenture to a single-instance global ERP platform in 2004-5 – initially for financial management, but eventually to encompass other business processes, such as human resources, sales, and legal.

With the IT function already showing measurable operational gains, we began in 2007 to switch our strategic focus to how we could help make Accenture more effective as an enterprise, while continuing to make the IT function more effective itself. A company-wide network transformation initiative set the stage by combining data and voice onto a single network, and dramatically increasing our bandwidth capacity. We launched a major effort to raise collaboration among Accenture professionals – a program that continues today. In areas from new business development to engagement management, we leveraged IT's power to craft new applications, which are helping Accenture professionals deliver more and higher quality services to Accenture clients by executing their work more efficiently and effectively.

The rework versus replace debate

At the outset of the decade, and at many points along the timeline, we found ourselves repeatedly coming up against the same core strategic decision: should we rework, or replace? When the time comes to upgrade equipment and systems, is it better to rework what you have – patching and tweaking systems and software to keep things running – or should you replace the old technology entirely and start with a clean IT slate?

This "rework versus replace" debate is familiar to every IT executive. Many businesses today are still using production software dating from decades past. A philosophy of "it works, so don't touch it" inevitably leads to hybrid IT environments, in which multiple conflicting systems co-exist, and documentation and qualified programmers are hard to find. It usually appears to be cheaper and always seems safer to patch than to risk transformational change. But is it?

Accenture's sudden creation as a free-standing company cast the issue in dramatic relief. Although we certainly did not plan it that way, our journey effectively became an accidental test of the "rework versus replace" debate. When we started, we did not intend to replace everything; but over time, we consistently chose to jettison the old in favor of the new. We did not want to be encumbered by the conflicts between old and new technologies, which impose massive burdens on business performance. Looking back over 10 years of work, we discovered that we changed absolutely everything. Today, the oldest application running in Accenture's production environment is just 10 years old – and we are replacing it.

Results to date

Figure 18 compares basic performance metrics for Accenture's IT operation today against our baseline year of 2001.

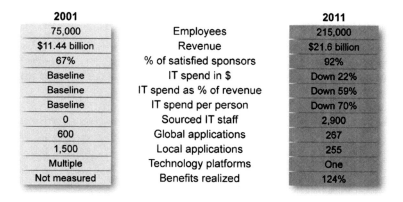

2001		2011
75,000	Employees	215,000
$11.44 billion	Revenue	$21.6 billion
67%	% of satisfied sponsors	92%
Baseline	IT spend in $	Down 22%
Baseline	IT spend as % of revenue	Down 59%
Baseline	IT spend per person	Down 70%
0	Sourced IT staff	2,900
600	Global applications	267
1,500	Local applications	255
Multiple	Technology platforms	One
Not measured	Benefits realized	124%

Figure 18: Accenture IT then and now

The comparison highlights the dramatic growth experienced by Accenture over this decade, as its workforce expanded from 75,000 to over 215,000 in 2011, and revenues nearly doubled to US$21.6 billion in 2011 from US$11.4 billion 10 years earlier.

Four key IT metrics reflect the results of running IT like a business:

- Our percentage of satisfied sponsors, as measured during our annual surveys, rose over the decade from 67%, in 2001, to 92% in 2011.
- Accenture's annual IT spend in terms of absolute dollars declined over the period by 22%, despite the fact that our workforce increased by nearly 300%.
- Accenture's annual IT spend as a percentage of company revenues declined by 59% over the period.
- Finally, Accenture's annual IT spend per person fell by 70%.

These metrics offer clear confirmation of the positive impact that a business approach to IT can have on user attitudes toward IT services, on IT's efficiency as a function, and on IT's ability to make significant contributions to bottom-line profits. Based on our audits of industry benchmarks, we can confidently say that, in terms of IT spending, Accenture's performance meets or beats the lowest readings for other IT operations of comparable size in the marketplace today.

Other statistics in Figure 18 track other changes to the way we organised IT over the course of the decade. When we began, all our resources were full-time employees of the internal IT function; by 2011, as many as 2,900 of our professionals were variable resources working in Accenture delivery centers off-shore, or consultants seconded to the IT function for a specific initiative. The 600 global applications we began the decade with had decreased to 267, and the 1,500 local applications had been reduced to 255, dramatically simplifying our operation and reducing the demand for skilled resources. Moving away from multiple technology platforms, we gradually standardized our operations on a single architecture platform – a simplification that delivered significant operational benefits. For those who believe in best-of-breed solutions, we point to these metrics as evidence that, in our experience and with very few exceptions, simpler is almost always better. Lastly, we have seen benefits realized exceed benefits expected by 124%. So not only were we able to confirm 100% delivery of the benefits promised by our IT investments, but we actually exceeded our own projected returns by 24%, as measured by the rigorous and independently audited tracking system described in Chapter 3.

Cost-benefit analysis

Accenture invested approximately US$1 billion in the hundreds of transformational projects and individual initiatives represented by the timeline shown earlier in Figure 17. If US$1 billion was the total cost of our transformational journey, what was the benefit? The metrics just outlined clearly confirm operational benefits and spending reductions. But what were the total dollar savings on Accenture's investment in high-performance IT?

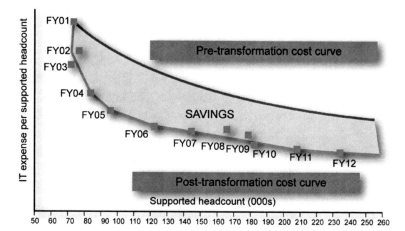

Figure 19: Accenture savings from IT investments

Figure 19 plots the savings over time resulting from Accenture's cumulative US$1 billion investment in transformational IT between fiscal year 2001 and the present day. The top line in this figure plots the IT expense per person supported, based on Accenture IT's pre-transformational operating model. If we had made no changes at all in our IT operations, and Accenture's workforce from 2001 through 2011 had grown as it did – from 75,000 to over 215,000 – we would have seen a gradual and entirely expected decline in the IT spend per employee; as the total workforce had expanded, the fixed cost portion of IT spending would have been distributed across a growing number of Accenture's professionals.

The bottom line in the same figure plots the actual IT expense per employee supported from fiscal years 2001 through 2011, with projections to fiscal year 2012 and beyond.

Once again, the total Accenture workforce over the current period will grow from 75,000 to over 215,000 – just as in the prior plotting. The quite dramatic declines in the early years, shown by the lower curve, reflect the success of our early efforts to run IT like a business. After fiscal year 2007, the declines were recorded at a more gradual pace, but they continued year after year, and will continue to save money for Accenture well into the future. We have moved the IT function to an entirely new cost curve.

The difference between the two lines – highlighted by the shaded area – represents the savings resulting from the transformational IT investments of approximately US$1 billion. In dollar terms, these savings total over US$3 billion for a three-to-one – or 300% – return on Accenture's investment in IT over the past 10 years.

Figure 20 provides a statistical snapshot of Accenture IT operations in the year 2011.

Hardware and network

- 196,000+ workstations deployed
- 6,013 devices monitored
- 4,372 servers managed
- 15,050 megabytes network bandwidth managed.

Websites

- 44,000 unique visitors to Accenture portal per day
- 27,000 unique visitors to www.accenture.com per day
- 95,000 unique visitors to Accenture People per month
- 57,000 views on Media Exchange per month
- 61,000 unique visits to the Knowledge Exchange per month
- 42,000 unique search queries per day.

Applications

- 267 global applications
- 255 local applications supported
- Single-instance global SAP ERP.

Collaboration

- 208,00 e-mail accounts
- 5,400,000 e-mail messages per day
- 27,000,000 spam messages blocked
- 5,000 Telepresence hours per month
- 45,000 PCs enabled with webcams
- 11,000 SharePoint® sites
- 75,000 mobile devices (iPhone®/BlackBerry®/Windows®)
- 45,000,000 audio conferencing minutes per month
- 24,000,000 Office Communicator (OC) instant messaging (IM) sessions per month
- 37,000,000 OC conference minutes per month
- 200,000 peer-to-peer OC video minutes per month
- 5,100 updates per month to Accenture People profiles
- 1,400+ communities of practice on the Knowledge Exchange.

Support

- 1,283,298 resolved incidents per year through help desk, self-service, web chat, local support
- 1,265,158 self-service contacts.

Figure 20: Accenture IT operations in 2011

Your transformational IT journey

Accenture's experience with IT transformation may be atypical, and there can be no assurance that every organization's IT transformation will be as productive as ours. The unusual circumstances of Accenture's creation in 2000-2001 provided us with a "burning platform" that forced decisions and actions. Now, as we look back over the ground we traversed, our results force us to conclude that, had we to do it all over again, we would do everything the same, only faster – so we could have realized the benefits sooner.

Whatever your situation, this much is beyond argument: the longer you retain obsolete technology, the more it drags down your performance, and the higher the price you will pay in innovations sacrificed; the faster you leverage the latest innovations in IT, the more you will benefit, and the sooner you will deliver the full advantages of high-performance IT to your organization.

You may well want to consider the promise of a transformational IT initiative, regardless of the size of your IT organization. Certainly, not every enterprise faces the urgency we felt to change the IT function from the foundations up. Different organizational structures will also have a bearing on how quickly or how radically you implement change. But even if your IT team chooses to pursue incremental rather than transformational changes, our experience does indicate that you can more than recover your investments in high-performance IT.

ITG RESOURCES

IT Governance Ltd. sources, creates and delivers products and services to meet the real-world, evolving IT governance needs of today's organizations, directors, managers and practitioners.

The ITG website (*www.itgovernance.co.uk*) is the international one-stop-shop for corporate and IT governance information, advice, guidance, books, tools, training and consultancy.

http://www.itgovernance.co.uk/it_governance.aspx is the page on our website for resources relevant to this book.

Other Websites

Books and tools published by IT Governance Publishing (ITGP) are available from all business booksellers and are also immediately available from the following websites:

www.itgovernance.co.uk/catalog/355 provides information and online purchasing facilities for every currently available book published by ITGP.

http://www.itgovernance.eu is our euro-denominated website which ships from Benelux and has a growing range of books in European languages other than English.

www.itgovernanceusa.com is a US$-based website that delivers the full range of IT Governance products to North America, and ships from within the continental US.

www.itgovernanceasia.com provides a selected range of ITGP products specifically for customers in South Asia.

www.27001.com is the IT Governance Ltd. website that deals specifically with information security management, and ships from within the continental US.

Pocket Guides

For full details of the entire range of pocket guides, simply follow the links at *www.itgovernance.co.uk/publishing.aspx*.

Toolkits

ITG's unique range of toolkits includes the IT Governance Framework Toolkit, which contains all the tools and guidance that you will need in order to develop and implement an appropriate IT governance framework for your organization. Full details can be found at *www.itgovernance.co.uk/ products/519*.

For a free paper on how to use the proprietary Calder-Moir IT Governance Framework, and for a free trial version of the toolkit, see *www.itgovernance.co.uk/calder_moir.aspx*.

There is also a wide range of toolkits to simplify implementation of management systems, such as an ISO/IEC 27001 ISMS or a BS25999 BCMS, and these can all be viewed and purchased online at: *http://www.itgovernance.co.uk/catalog/1*.

Best Practice Reports

ITG's range of Best Practice Reports is now at *www.itgovernance.co.uk/best-practice-reports.aspx*. These offer you essential, pertinent, expertly researched information on a number of key issues including Web 2.0 and Green IT.

ITG Resources

Training and Consultancy

IT Governance also offers training and consultancy services across the entire spectrum of disciplines in the information governance arena. Details of training courses can be accessed at *www.itgovernance.co.uk/training.aspx* and descriptions of our consultancy services can be found at *http://www.itgovernance.co.uk/consulting.aspx*. Why not contact us to see how we could help you and your organization?

Newsletter

IT governance is one of the hottest topics in business today, not least because it is also the fastest moving, so what better way to keep up than by subscribing to ITG's free monthly newsletter *Sentinel*? It provides monthly updates and resources across the whole spectrum of IT governance subject matter, including risk management, information security, ITIL and IT service management, project governance, compliance and so much more. Subscribe for your free copy at: *www.itgovernance.co.uk/newsletter.aspx*.

CPSIA information can be obtained at www.ICGtesting.com
Printed in the USA
BVOW011626180412

288019BV00003B/3/P